AL-FARD

THE DAWN

By

Ali Mahdi Muhammad

All Rights Reserved. No part of this book may be reproduced or transmitted in any form by any means, electronic, photocopying, mechanical, recording, information storage or retrieval system without permission from the publisher, The New World Nation of Islam. Brief quotations may be used interviews or commentary. None of the material in this writing can be reproduced without written permission from Allah in Muhammad Speaks..

The New World Nation of Islam
PO Box 8466
Newark, New Jersey 07108
www.thenewworldnationofislam.com
email: secretary@newworldnationislam.com

Copyright 2018 © by The New World Nation of Islam
Al-Fard: The Dawn
1st Printing November 1963

ISBN 13-digit 978-19477321-7-9 (Paperback)
ISBN 13-digit 978-19477321-8-6 (Hardback)
ISBN 13-digit 978-19477321-9-3 (E-book)

Library of Congress Catalog Number: 2018936574

1. Elijah Muhammad, Black Muslims, Nation of Islam, Islam, Islam in North America, New World Nation of Islam, Muslims, F.O.I., M.G.T & G.C.C.

Cover design by Nuance Art, LLC
Interior book design by Nuance Art
nuanceart@acreativenuance.com

Editorial Team: Nobel Ali, Samataha Ali, M. Ali
Printed in United States

ALI MAHDI MUHAMMAD

AL-FARD *THE DAWN*

A.M. MUHAMMAD
FIELD SUPREME MINISTER OF THE HONORABLE ELIJAH MUHAMMAD

WRITE OR SEND DONATIONS TO: THE NEW WORLD NATION OF ISLAM
PO BOX 8466 | NEWARK | NEW JERSEY 07108

SEND DONATIONS VIA PAYPAL: DONATENEWWORLD@GMAIL.COM

WWW.THENEWWORLDNATIONOFISLAM.COM

ALI MAHDI MUHAMMAD

DEDICATION

This Book is a Declaration of the Dawn, or the Advent of Muhammad's Day. This Announcement puts an end to the devil's Civilization.

This Book is Dedicated to the Trees of the Lord, planted in the Field, The Ministers of God, my Brothers and fellow servants, who through trials and tribulation have become CRYSTALLIZED in our Lord and Saviour, Jesus Christ. May the peace and mercy of Allah, forever be with Him.

As-Salaam Alaikum
Your Brother,
Muhammad Ali

In the Name of Allah, The Beneficent, The Merciful in the Person of Master Fard Muhammad, The Great Mahdi. And In the name of Our Father, The Most Honorable Mr. Elijah Muhammad, The Last God of the Old World and the First God of the New World Nation of Islam.

Peace! Peace!

Dear Believers,

According to the instructions of our Father, The Most Honorable Mr. Elijah Muhammad, we cannot sell the truth. It must be given freely as it is our divine right and heritage.

The price of this item is your donation to help pay the cost of producing our New World literature.

The receipt received from your purchase can be refunded in full cost after the establishment of the 1st National Bank and Treasury.

May Allah bless us all!

Peace! Peace!

Your Brother,

Ali Mahdi Muhammad

Ali Muhammad

P.S. Address all correspondence to:

Ali Mahdi Muhammad
P.O. Box 8466
Newark, NJ 07108

In the Name of Our Father, The Most Honorable Mr. Elijah Muhammad, The One God to Whom All Praise Is Due Forever. We Thank Allah, In the Person of Master Fard Muhammad For His Perfect Slave, Our Lord Muhammad. We the True Believers of Allah And This Day Of Judgement In Which We Now Live Greet You In Our New World Nation Of Islam's Greetings Of Peace To You In The Old World And Peace To You In The New World Hereafter . . . Peace! Peace!

"THE INTRODUCTION"

By Major Muntaqim Ali Allah

This book was written and prepared by the finger of Allah. It is a light and a guidance for all of those who hold dear to the teachings of the Most Honorable Elijah Muhammad (peace and blessings be upon Him and may He forever be one with Allah).

The Al-Fard, or the The Dawn, has captured the early rays of our history. This history is essential if we are to be brought face to face with the One true and living God of the universe. The purpose of this writing is to bring the reader step by step, one degree at a time to the reality of God in person. The teachings of our Father elevates the believer to the level of Godhood by teaching you to look for the God within as well as the God without. You become the God you worship. This book will take you through the great Transitions of power that each God goes through on His ascension to the throne.

When you read this book you will be filled with an Inspirational spirit, a spirit that will awaken in you the characteristics of a Shabazzian, the master builder. You will find your Identity, your purpose in life, the moment you begin to look pass the veil of ignorance and into the ever living light that the Blackman is God.

You, who are the sons and daughters of the Most Honorable Elijah Muhammad, your spiritual insight has never been destroyed by the years of miseducation, suffering and brutality. Thus, when you read these words of truth, you are resurrected from the grave, not a physical grave, but a mental grave of ignorance.

I urge you, my Brothers and Sisters to read this book in the name of Allah, just as the first revelation sent down to the prophet Muhammad of 1400 years ago, by the Angel Gabriel was to read in the Name of Allah (Holy Qur'an 96:1), I encourage you to read this scripture as if Allah had spoken directly to your heart.

The author of this book is a man of Divine Inspiration and Guidance. Ali Mahdi Muhammad, for the last 31 years has given life to an entire nation of Blackmen and women from the darkness of his prison cell. I ask you, what kind of man could hold on so long and so faithfully without turning his back on His Father's instructions? What kind of leader would sacrifice His all for the betterment of His people at this cost? . . . Read the Al-Fard and you will discover the answer to this question and more. Read the Al-Fard and see for yourself the history of the making of a nation and the transition of power of Allah from one God to another. This book produces true Executioners of the Will of God. Read it in the Name Of Allah and come into your own.

Peace! Peace!

TABLE OF CONTENTS

"THE INTRODUCTION"... x
OPENING 3
Chapter One WHO IS GOD? 9
Chapter Two WHO IS THE MESSENGER? 24
Chapter Three WHO ARE THE DISCIPLES? 45
A GUIDE TO UNDERSTANDING THE BIBLE AND HOLY QUR'AN 54
"THE HOLY QUR'AN"... 57
"A GUIDE TO UNDERSTANDING MESSAGE TO THE BLACKMAN".... 58
Mr. Muhammad Speaks February 3, 1962 60
Mr. Muhammad Speaks March 11, 1967 63
Mr. Muhammad Speaks March 18, 1967 65
Mr. Muhammad Speaks March 25, 1967 67
Mr. Muhammad Speaks June 10, 1967 70
Mr. Muhammad Speaks October 29, 1965 73
Mr. Muhammad Speaks July 15, 1966 75
Mr. Muhammad Speaks March 29, 1962 76
Mr. Muhammad Speaks June 16, 1967 78
Mr. Muhammad Speaks October 20, 1956 81
Mr. Muhammad Speaks 85
Mr. Muhammad Speaks 88
Mr. Muhammad Speaks August 8, 1964 91
Mr. Muhammad Speaks February 19, 1966 94

10/8/1967

Bis-mi-illah. Muhammad-Rasul-illah.

The darkest hour is just before Dawn: therefore, it is understood by the wise, the reason for the great misunderstanding and confusion regarding the coming of Master Fard Muhammad.

Allah, God, and His Prophet, the Messiah, is now in our midst. The Light of Supreme Truth is knocking the brains out of falsehood, and declaring that this great light is here to stay.

This writing attempts to retain some of these early rays that are now present showing the dawn of our day. The Wisdom, Knowledge and Understanding found in the following pages are in no way all of the light, it is only an idea of the great truth that is on the way: It does not mean that this little light has no value, in fact if you cannot accept what you find in this writing you will surely burn in hell. If you reject the little, you also reject the all.

In this writing, only three subjects are treated:

Chapter One: "Who Is Allah?" Which deals with the reality of the Supreme Being in our midst. Also, His work of resurrecting the prophet and teaching the Mahdi how to bring about a New World.

The second chapter deals with: "Who is The Messenger?" We try to show the Mahdi in the true light, how He is raised from the dead by Allah, and how He fulfills the prophecy of Moses, Jesus, Muhammad and the Lamb.

The last chapter: "Who Are The Disciples?" Deals with the Islamic Scientists, and the work they do under the direction of the Mahdi.

The fourth section of this writing contains foot-notes, which are the author's explanation and references for further study. The foot-notes are numerically out-lined in the same order as the verses to make study easy.

All the material found in the three chapters and verses, are quotes from the mouth of the Most Honorable Elijah Muhammad, and the references are the Holy Qur'an, the Bible, and the Book Message To The Blackman: and other articles written by Mr. Muhammad, what the author has experienced; that which the author has been taught by Master Fard Muhammad - make up the sum of this little book.

The author prays that this work will reflect the light of his Leader, Teacher, Prophet and Guide, Master Fard Muhammad. To this end I continue to labor.

Muhammad Ali,

Field Supreme Captain and Spokesman for the Prophet, and fellow servant of Allah.

As-Salaam Alaikum

Bis-mi-illah

OPENING

Know This And Be Wise. Be Comforted By The Comforter.

If you have eyes, then you should see! If you have ears, then you should hear! If you can read, then you should understand! Revelation 11:15, & Revelation 10:5-10.

"And the seventh angel sounded; and there were great voices in heaven, saying, The kingdoms of this world are become the kingdoms of our Lord, and of His Christ; and he shall reign forever and ever." And the angel which I saw stand upon the sea and upon the earth lifted up his hand to heaven. And sware by him that liveth forever and ever, who created heaven, and the things that therein are, and the earth, and the things that therein are, and the sea, and the things which are therein, But in the days of the voice of the seventh angel, when he shall begin to sound, the mystery of God should be finished, as he hath declared to his servants the prophets. And the voice which I heard from heaven spake unto me again, and said, Go and take the little book which is open in the hand of the angel which standeth upon the sea and upon the earth. And I went unto the angel, and said unto him, Give me the little book. And he said unto me. Take it, and eat it up; and it shall make thy belly bitter, but it shall be in thy mouth sweet as honey: and as soon as I had eaten it, my belly was bitter."

Peace . . . Peace . . .

Muhammad Ali
Spokesman for the Prophet

Chapter One

WHO IS ALLAH?

In the Name of Allah, the Beneficent, the Most Merciful, Master of the Day of Judgment, to Him alone do we submit and seek refuge. Say: Allah, bears witness that there is no God, but He, and so does the angels and those possessed of knowledge maintaining justice. There is no God, but He and we bear witness that Muhammad, is His servant and Messenger. And we believe in him and honor him and help him and follow the light sent down with him: and we hear and obey. Our Lord, Thy forgiveness do we crave and to Thee, is our eventual course.

Quote: The Honorable, Mr. Elijah Muhammad, said:

(1) "I have been made equal in knowledge with Allah. I have power over the Sun, Moon and Stars. I control the winds and seas. I have waited over 379 years for this day." (Foot-note #1)

(2) "Though I might seem insignificant to you nevertheless, I am the man." (Foot-note #2)

(3) "God blessed Chicago with a good, mild winter because I have been in your midst. I was commissioned by Allah, to prophecy. I'm the Last Messenger - don't look for another one. Behind Me comes God;" (Foot-note #3)

(4) "The Spirit of Life is and has been with us all of our lives. God is in person among us today. He is a man, He is in His time. God sees, hears, knows, wills, acts and is a person. Man." (Foot-note #4)

(5) "Both the Bible and Holy Qur'an, teach of the presence of God in person at the end of the world of satan, the devils rule. We would be foolish to disbelieve that such character is not present and is not directing the course of the nation's today." (Foot-note #5)

(6) "My grandfather gave me the name Elijah. My last name was Poole. Allah asked me to change to Muhammad. Allah, suggested later that I take Abdul, but Abdul stands opposed to what I stand for." (Foot-note #6)

(7) "The true religion of Islam is being offered for the first time to us, the lost-found members of our nation, by God Himself." (Foot-note #7)

(8) "The man Allah (God) raised from among the American so-called Negroes in the West will unite His people with the guidance of Allah, with a book of scripture for his people prepared and written by the finger of Allah." (Foot-note #8)

(9) "This question (Who is the Original Man?) is being answered from the mouth of Allah (God) to us the so-called Negroes for the first time since our straying away from our own nation." (Foot-note #9)

(10) "The Day has come that all mankind must know the reality of Allah, God. There can be no Judgment of the people until this knowledge has been given to the people." (Foot-note #10)

Chapter Two

WHO IS THE MESSENGER?

(1) "Who is His Father, if God, is not His father? God is His father, but the Father is also a man." (Foot-note #11)

(2) "The Great Mahdi, this is the fulfillment of the prophecy of the coming of the Son of Man, the Great Messiah. This is the second coming." (Foot-note #12)

(3) "I shall continue to warn you of the penalty that awaits you who rejects your God and my Saviour, Master Fard Muhammad." (Foot-note #13)

(4) "Glorify Thy Son, that Thy Son may Glorify Thee." (Foot-note #14)

(5) "You have two Jesus histories, as I have said time and again, and even an Apostle's history of the last days, all under the name of Jesus, of 2,000 years ago." (Foot-note #15)

(6) "The Great Mahdi has taken Fard as a name for himself corresponding with the time of his coming - which is the early days (or years) of the seven thousand years and the year under the name Millennium (Which the Christians say means the 1,000 years Christ will reign on the earth.)" (Foot-note #16)

(7) "(144,000) This number is mentioned in the Bible, Rev. 14:1, as being the First Believers in Allah God, and His Messenger. The Messenger is called the Lamb due to certain characteristics of His God." (Foot-note #17)

(8) "In Revelations, the symbolic Lamb in the midst of four- beast.

All the scholars and scientists of the (white race) know this is not referring to Muhammad 1,400 years ago." (Foot-note #18)

(9) "The story of Moses and the Pharaoh is a warning to you today." (Foot-note #19)

(10) "I think it is time for Elijah, to go back to the prison to raise some more good Ministers." (Foot-note #20)

Chapter Three

WHO ARE THE DISCIPLES?

(1) "They make statues of Jesus and His twelve disciples, although they have never had a true picture, or true piece of sculpture of them, as there was none available in that day and time." (Foot-note #21)

(2) "There are religious scientist in Islam, who know these things to be true that I am saying." (Foot-note #22)

(3) "When such history is written, it is done by twenty-four (24) Scientists." (Foot-note #23)

(4) "He (the Lamb) gets the name (praised) from the honor of twenty-four elders, or Islamic Scientists." (Foot-note #24)

(5) "The Executioners are on the way." (Foot-note #25)

Chapter One
WHO IS GOD?

Foot-note #1

February 26, 1960, at the Saviour's Day Convention in Chicago Illinois, during Mr. Muhammad's speech, he revealed this great light and truth. This light was so bright, it blinded some of the followers. The author witnessed some people walking out of the audience indignant toward what they heard. Obviously, these indignant followers did not believe in the first principle of Islam, which is, the belief in the One True, and Living God, Who has no equal.

Holy Qur'an Chapter 112: THE UNITY.

"In the name of Allah, the Beneficent, the Merciful.

Say: He, Allah, is One. Allah is He on Whom all depend. He begets not, nor is He begotten; And none is like Him."

Also, Holy Bible - Psalms 82: "God standeth in the congregation of the mighty; he judgeth among the gods, etc." Exodus 29:45, "And I will dwell among the children of Israel and will be their God." Numbers 16:3, "And they gathered themselves together against Moses and Aaron and said unto them, ye take too much upon you, seeing all the congregation are holy, every one of them, and the Lord is among them: wherefore then lift ye up yourselves above the congregation of the Lord. Exodus 6:7, "And I will take you to me for a people, and I will be to you a God, and ye shall know that I am the Lord your God," etc.

Neither Moses or Aaron is God Allah; but Moses is Allah's last and greatest prophet and Aaron is the Spokesman for Moses. All three are in the congregation of our people today, the so-called American Negro. Allah is and always has been among His people, the Holy Tribe of Shabazz. He is the Creator of the worlds, and the life that exist in them. He creates what we should think and how we should act, what we should eat. Also, the clothes we wear are also the creation of Allah. His is the power to make whom He please great, so He creates angels and men. His wisdom encompasses all things.

Foot-note #2

It was in the fall of 1958, in the city of Boston, that the author first heard this statement though it has been repeated since then. The author recalls being in the audience and seeing and hearing Mr. Muhammad for the first time. It was an electrifying experience. Mr. Muhammad taught Jesus' history as if he were remembering the events as they actually took place, giving the author the impression that he had been with Jesus during that time. "Though I might seem insignificant to you, nevertheless, I am the man," fits the prophecy of John the Baptist perfectly. Whenever John the Baptist was questioned about his authority he would say, that he was only the Messenger of Allah. "The voice crying in the wilderness." John said that he was looking for and preparing the way for the Mahdi; who he said was greater, or of more significance than himself. St. John 1:19, 34. "And this is the record of John, when the Jews sent priests and Le'vites from Jerusalem to ask him, Who art thou? And he confessed, and denied not; but confessed, I am not the Christ. And they asked him, What then? Art thou Eli'as? And he saith, I am not. Art thou that Prophet? ' And he answered, No. Then said they unto him, Who art thou? That we may give an answer to them that sent us. What sayest thou of thyself? He said, I am the voice of one crying in the wilderness. Make straight the way of the Lord, as said the prophet E-sa'ias. And they which were sent were of the Pharisees. And they asked him, and said unto him, Why baptizest thou then, if thou be not that Christ, nor Elias, neither that Prophet? John answered them, saying, I baptize with water: but there standeth one among you, whom ye know not; He it is, who coming after me is preferred before me, whose shoe's-latchet I am not worthy to unloose. These things were done in Bethabara beyond Jordan, where John was baptizing. The next day John seeth Jesus coming unto him, and saith, "Behold the lamb of God, which taketh away the sin of the world! This is he of whom I said, After me cometh a man which is preferred before me; for he was before me. And I knew him not: but that he should be made manifest to Israel, therefore am I come baptizing with water. And John bare record, saying I saw the Spirit descending from heaven like a dove, and it abode upon him." (The author was present to witness the fulfillment of the recognition of the Mahdi, November or December 1958 in the city of Newark, New Jersey.) "And I knew him not, but he that sent me to baptize with water, the same said unto me, upon whom thou shalt see the Spirit descending and remaining on him, the same is he which baptizeth with the Holy Ghost. And I saw, and bore record that this is the Son of God." This prophecy is a perfect picture of the Most Hon. Elijah Muhammad. He is the voice in the wilderness. For 28 years He taught that righteousness is the key. To repent of the evil way of life, and make ready to meet the Saviour. Mr. Muhammad, knew that the Saviour would one day come to Him from among our people (Tribe of Shabazz), and that He, Mr. Elijah Muhammad, would be the only one to recognize Him. This, the author bears witness that He, Mr. Elijah Muhammad, did November or December 1958 at the Rickery Auditorium in Newark, New Jersey. This was the first visit of Mr. Muhammad, to teach His new followers. He came to Newark against the advice of His doctor and family. He had a very high temperature above 100 degrees, but He said that Allah told Him to deliver the message no matter what; so, He caught a plane and came anyway. As He began to teach He said that He did not feel sick anymore, that He was feeling most happy. Then He looked out into the audience and said, "I see Allah, don't you see Him? No, I don't guess you can, not yet." Of course, the author was looking all over the place, but couldn't recognize Allah: just as Mr. Muhammad had said, not at that time. Mr. Muhammad went on explaining how He felt no more sickness and was so happy because this was the day He had waited 379 years for. He said that He was giving us a Mosque Number 25, and said that 25 was His number and that this was His Mosque, the Model Mosque. He led the closing prayer himself. The Christ had been recognized, but only Mr. Muhammad saw Him at that time. Yet, Mr. Muhammad claimed to be insignificant. Jesus' first work, (according to Matt. 11) was to reveal just who John the Baptist really was. Jesus, after being baptized by John, began to teach John's doctrine, "Repent the time of this world is at hand." Jesus also taught that all praise are due to his father. He was not referring to Joseph, his physical father, but the father who gave him spiritual life, or awakening, his spiritual father, the God of the living. Jesus says, St. Luke 10:22-24, "All things are delivered to me of my Father; and no man knoweth who the Son is, but the Father; and who the Father is, but the Son, and he to whom the Son will reveal him. And Jesus turned to his disciples and said privately, "Blessed are the eyes which see the things that ye (my disciples) see. For I tell you that many prophets and Kings have desired to see those things which ye see, and have not seen them, and to hear these things which ye hear, and have not heard them," Jesus still speaking of John the Baptist, Matt. 11:13,14, "For all the prophets and the law prophesied until John. And if you will receive it, this is Elias, which was to come." In verse 9 of the same chapter Jesus says that John was more than just a prophet.

Foot-Note #3

(For power of Sun, Moon and Stars, see foot-note one.)

Last Messenger? First consider that all scriptures teach that God is a man who comes at the end of the wicked world, to gather His chosen people. He is unknown although He is seen and heard by everyone. John the Baptist and Elijah are the same person. It is a great mistake to interpret the prophecy of John to refer to the past (2,000 years ago). It is made clear in the chapter 4:5 of Malachi, that Elijah comes at the judgement of this world. What is the great mystery about the identity of Elijah or John? Why does the officials want to know His true identity? Why does Jesus question His disciples about Elijah's identity? Read St. John, first chapter, it makes the truth plain to see. The voice crying in the wilderness was the God, who created a world or nation of his people. But His people knew him not. But whoever would recognize Him (His true identity) would receive the power to become the Son of God. Jesus was the first to see God, therefore, He is the Mahdi, the Son of Man, and we can understand Him saying, "All praise is due to My Father. Elijah, glorifies the Mahdi and calls Him his Lord, just as David called His son Solomon, Lord. Solomon built the temple or kingdom of His Father's desire. The Mahdi builds the kingdom of Elijah's desire.

Foot-note #4

This statement can be found in an article in the book Message To The Blackman, page 13,14 and 15. The opening statement of this article, "The Coming of Allah God" says, that only a few people know the mystery of Allah, being among us. Also, page 73 of the same book says, "But until today, the true knowledge of the One, Divine Supreme Being, is known only to a few." Let us understand that there is only one God. Even though two Gods are predicted to show at the end of the wicked world. The first God is Allah who establishes a world or nation of people, and prepares them to meet His Spokesman, the Holy One, or the Great Mahdi. Allah, must prepare the way for His Prophet, because the prophet has no divine power of his own. And if Allah, God, does not protect the Holy One, the prophet, Master Fard Muhammad, the devil will destroy this Holy Prophet as he, the devil, has done to many of the past. Read the article "God Came From Teman and the Holy One from Mt. Paran." We must know that the prophecy of Jesus and Moses does not refer to the past, but is showing the work of the Mahdi in the last days. The Mahdi has no choice as to whether he will be Allah's prophet or not. Allah raises him, teaches Him Islam, and tells him how to fight for the freedom of his people. Therefore, Allah calls His Spiritual Son, God, Allah in the person of Master Fard Muhammad. But both these Gods bear witness that Allah is One and the Father of us all. Allah, comes first to tell us that His judgment has come and that we must repent, because His prophet who comes after Him, must activate His warnings. Allah or Jehovah, was already in the land among the Israelites when He called Moses to inform him that he was the prophet. Allah was already in the land when Jesus received his mission. Allah is always first. But you must understand that no one knows the identity of Allah until the prophet meets Him and receives his mission to bring an end to a wicked civilization. This has always been the course of Allah and it is the same today. The mystery of God and new revelations concerning Allah's Kingdom, comes with the prophet, the Great Mahdi.

Read your Holy Qur'an, chapter 7:11-14. It shows that when Adam was raised or created, there was already a nation that Allah had informed of the coming of the one He, Allah, was creating (Adam). Allah called all to submit to his prophet, but some (Iblis the devil) would not submit. Allah has always been among his people the Tribe of Shabazz. Read "The Origin of God Being a Spirit and Not a Man", page 8, Message To The Blackman. Well, we all know that there was a God in the beginning that created all these things and we do know that He does not exist today. But we know again that from that God the person of God continued until today in His people, and today a Supreme One (God) has appeared among us with the same infinite wisdom to bring about a complete change.

Foot-note #5

This statement is taken from an article Mr. Muhammad Speaks, February 3, 1962, entitled "THE END". Here in the plainest of words we are told that Allah is among the so-called Negroes today. We are the Holy Tribe of Shabazz, the Family of Allah. This is why we had to suffer the most, and become the least of people in the eyes of the civilized world: to be redeemed only at the end of the wicked world, or the resurrection. Allah, first comes to the so-called Negro, and gives us the Supreme Wisdom, which has been hidden from the world that He is our God and we are His people (Family) and He Allah, is a man and has always been among us, His people. The Judgment Day, or the Day of the Lord, means the days or years that Allah reveals Himself among His people, along with His Last and Greatest Prophet, to the world. All the prophets of the old knew that Allah would be in person among His people at the Great Resurrection, of the Day of the Lord. Read Joel 2:27, and 3:17, "And ye shall know that I am in the midst of Israel, and that I am the Lord your God, and none else, and my people shall never be ashamed." Here in Joel, we find Allah, taking His people out of the hands of their slave masters and elevating His people to a position of dignity so that we have nothing else to be ashamed of. 3:17, "So shall you know that I am the Lord your God dwelling in Zion, my Holy Mountain. Then shall Jerusalem be holy and there shall no strangers pass through her anymore." Here it shows that Allah Himself, must clean up the Holy City, before He can reside there. Allah in person says, 3:7, "Behold I will raise them out of a place where you have sold them and will return your recompense upon your own head." Could this be a spirit? No! this is Allah. Why can't we see who is independently in our midst? Who is most wise in our midst? Who is our only source of life? The man in our midst who has power to resurrect the dead, is Allah. It is God's word only, that puts life back into the dry bones. Read Ezekiel 37:3-4. This prophecy is beautiful, in that it shows how Allah is present among His people and has many helpers or angels. But these helpers are not Allah's choice of a Messenger, so Allah raises Ezekiel and teaches him what Allah desires for him to do, and then Allah brings about His will, the resurrection of the dead and the judgment. "And He said unto me, Son of Man, can these bones live? And I answered, O Lord God, thou knowest. Again, he said unto me, prophecy upon these bones, and say unto them, O ye dry bones, hear the word of the Lord."

The Son of Man doesn't speak for Himself, he speaks the words of the Lord. Master Fard Muhammad doesn't speak his own words, but he speaks all His Father, Allah, in person taught him. Allah's words in our midst today is what is giving life to the dead. All prophets bear witness that only Allah in person at the end of the wicked world can give life to a dead nation and make them the head instead of the tail. Allah always uses a prophet to reveal Himself.

Foot-note #6

This statement is taken from an interview with Mr. Muhammad in the book Black Nationalism. Remember that we have two histories of Fard. One is past, the other is now being fulfilled. This statement is referring to the Great Angel, who came in 1930, looking for his uncle the Lord of all the Worlds. This angel brought with him the keys and a crown of life and gave them to the rightful owner,

Elijah. This Great Angel then left the work of establishing the Kingdom of God, and the resurrection of the dead for Elijah to do. This Great Angel plays the part of Joseph, in the history of Jesus, and Elijah has the part of Mary, Jesus' mother. Read Holy Qur'an 19:17 to 21. "So she screened herself from them. Then we sent to her our spirit and it appeared to her in the form of a well made man. She said, I flee for refuge from thee to the Beneficent, if thou art the one guarding against evil. He said I am only a bearer of a message of thy Lord: That I will give thee a pure boy. She said, how can I have a son and no mortal has touched me, nor have I been unchaste? He said, so it will be. Thy Lord says, it is easy to me, and that we will make him a sign to man and a mercy from us. And it is a matter decreed." Sociology refers to nations as her, so this is our reason for showing Elijah as Mary and the mother of the second coming of Jesus. Also read Holy Qur'an 3:44, "When the angels said: O Mary, surely Allah gives thee good news with a word from Him (of one) whose name is the Messiah, Jesus, son of Mary, worthy of regard in this world and the Hereafter, and of those who are drawn nigh (to Allah). The above shows that the Great Angel who came to Elijah, in 1930, and revealed to Elijah what was decreed or written, had no choice in the matter. This Angel came in the name of Allah as it is stated above to give Elijah news that He, Elijah would give spiritual birth to the Last and Greatest Prophet the world has ever known. The Messiah, Christ, the Mahdi and Master Fard Muhammad are the same man. All these names refer to the Prophet Elijah raised from among our people. Muslim means, one who submits entirely to Allah. Abdul, means servant of Allah. The Creator of all the Prophets and all that is, cannot be Abdul, it is opposed to what Almighty God Allah, stands for. History shows that the coming of the Great Angel in 1930 and his staying 3 1/2 years, coincides with Joseph visiting Mary and putting on the disguise of Mary's father, so as to fool the enemy. This is also the case when Mr. Fard met with Elijah, from 1930 to 1934.

Foot-note #7

This statement is taken from an article of Mr. Muhammad Speaks, "Islam Means Unity", June 10, 1967. "For trillions of years the true identity of Allah has been a mystery, Islam is the religion of Allah and has been taught by all the prophets. But Islam was not to be perfected until God came Himself at the end of the wicked world. Read Holy Qur'an 5:3, "This day have I perfected for you your religion and completed My favor to you and chosen for you Islam as a religion." Today we the Lost Found members of the Tribe of Shabazz, are receiving the Supreme Wisdom from Allah Himself. No other nation has this divine truth. All Islamic Nations are believers in a spirit God. These nations believe that Allah is a spirit in the heavens above somewhere, and that the Great Mahdi, will come in these last days. But they don't know from where, or from what nation of people. They don't want to believe that Allah is with us and has raised the Mahdi from among us, the Lost Tribe of God, so-called Negroes. So, we who have been deprived of Islam for 400 years must now teach the world what Allah in our midst has taught us.

Foot-note #8

This statement comes from the article Mr. Muhammad Speaks, "The Truth (part 6) March 29, 1962. Mr. Muhammad has taught for 36 years the coming of the Son of Man, the Mahdi, just as John the Baptist taught for such a long time in the wilderness, the coming of Christ. Elijah says that the Mahdi will come and take a new book of scripture with the new divine knowledge and guidance of Allah and build the New World. It is plainly stated that the Messiah is raised from among the so-called Negroes. It is foolish for you to think that the Mahdi came and did this in the years from 1930 to 1934. If Fard of 1930 was Allah and Mr. Muhammad as the Lamb, the Christ, or the last and Greatest Prophet raised from among us to guide us eastward with the new book of God, and establish the kingdom of Allah, why has He taught you and I for 36 years that the Son of Man would do this, and we must wait until He comes? You have never heard Mr. Muhammad say that He is the Christ or the Last Prophet, the Lamb. The Christ is under the authority of his Father! This is not Elijah, there is none in the heavens or the earth greater than Elijah! Mr. Fard of 1930 came from another country, and we are warned against looking for anyone coming other than from us, the so-called Negroes. Read Rev. 5, it shows how God, Allah is present and with Him are many helpers (angels) and four beasts. Allah has in His hand a book written by His fingers that none of those helper's present could qualify to open. Therefore, Allah raises one from among the dead. The Lamb, Christ, or the Mahdi, and gave Him the book. This makes the Lamb the last and greatest prophet and spokesman for Allah, not Allah, because Allah is the one who raised him from the dead! Allah is all wise and has the keys to life and death, heaven and hell. He is He who was dead and is alive forever more, the first and last, the beginning and the end, and He has always been among us teaching and preparing us for this great day. Try to understand that there would be no need for Mr. Muhammad to teach the coming of the Mahdi, if the Mahdi had already come, or if as some believe, that He is the Mahdi, the Christ. Mr. Muhammad did not receive any new book written by the finger of the Great Angel, Fard of 1930. Nor did that Angel prepare the way by teaching the coming of Elijah. Elijah did not need any new book. Elijah recognized the Angel Fard, of 1930, as soon as he saw Him, because He, Elijah was waiting for Him. Mr. Muhammad has written a new book, revealing the true identity of Allah and His Last Prophet, whom He raises in the last days. And only the first begotten of the dead, so-called Negro (the Mahdi) can receive this book and put it into action. The great Angel Fard of 1930, was never mentally dead, nor was He a so-called Negro of the Tribe of Shabazz. He was half and half. Nor was the Angel, Fard to live forever; He is to live 410 years! May the peace and blessing of Allah forever be upon this Great Angel, who came in the Name of Allah and in the Person of Master Fard Muhammad.

Foot-note #9

This statement comes out of Supreme Wisdom No. 2, chapter two page 7. "The aboriginal people are none other than the Tribe of Shabazz, the so- called American Negro." Read Message To The Blackman, page 31, where it states, "It is Allah's (God's) will and purpose that we shall know ourselves." In the same paragraph it also says, "Who is better knowing of who we are than God, Himself." He has declared that we are the descendants of the Asiatic Black Nation and of the Tribe of Shabazz." Again, in the same article, "So, being the first and smartest scientist on the deportation of our moon and the one who suffered the most of all, Allah God, has decided to place us on top with a thorough knowledge of self and His guidance." This is the teaching of Mr. Muhammad, out of His own mouth. Just as the prophecy says, He would teach in the wilderness for 40 years. Read your Bible and see how perfectly the prophecy fits Allah's work in our midst. Deuteronomy 8:2, "And thou shalt remember all the ways which the Lord thy God led thee these forty years in the wilderness, to humble thee, and to prove thee, to know what was in thine heart, whether thou wouldest keep His commandments, or not." Mr. Muhammad has been teaching for 36 years as of June 1967. Read the article Mr. Muhammad Speaks, "THE TIME AND WHAT MUST BE DONE" June 16, 1967. "I want you to remember that I have always taught that you should return to your God, and people." Also, in the same article it says, "The day of which I have been warning you for 36 years is here." Also read the article "MY MISSION is to give life." Mr. Muhammad was asked "How would you describe your mission? (answer) "My mission is to give life to the dead. What I teach brings them out of death and into life." Allah is the possessor of power over all things and He alone can raise the dead. Read Holy Qur'an chapter 22:7, "And the hour is coming, there is no doubt about it; and Allah will raise up those who are in the graves." The graves here mentioned is referring to a mental grave of ignorance, not a physical grave.

Foot-note #10

This statement comes out of Message To The Blackman page 13. Here is a powerful statement showing much light on what and when judgment is. "There can be no judgment until the reality of Allah is made known to the people." Allah, never reveals Himself to the people. He always raises a prophet from among the people Allah intends to judge. The people are then judged according to their acceptance of the true identity of - the reality of Allah, as taught by the prophet from among them. Mr. Muhammad has taught us for 36 years that this perfect knowledge of the reality of Allah, would come with the Mahdi, not the one who came in 1930. It is a mistake to think that judgment took place 37 years ago. Mr. Muhammad says that the Saviour is now born in our midst, meaning Jesus, the Great Mahdi, who is now teaching the truth of Allah. It is not for Allah to reveal Himself to the people, so He keeps the secret and lets the prophet give the people this perfect and unequaled guidance. Allah's Kingdom is built by the Saviour, and only those who accept the truth of the reality of Allah as taught by the Saviour, will be members of the New World of Allah. This is why we are taught by Allah to wait for the Mahdi, the Son of Man. Read your Bible. John the Baptist taught his Nation of Islam, that they would not know who would be saved until Jesus had come.

So, they had to wait not knowing who would enter the Kingdom of God: though many had followed John the Baptist for many years, still their salvation depends on their acceptance of Jesus. This is because Jesus was to tell all of the truth, which was to be a new song. Notice that when John raised Jesus, he, Jesus, began to teach "that John is the greatest" and all of the praise was due to his (Jesus) heavenly Father. Jesus had to get out on his own because the followers of John, who were in position of authority in the nation's Mosques were against Jesus. Jesus had to raise his own followers in the field, because they had no Mosque, so it is today. Judgment comes when Allah raises the Mahdi, from among the so-called Negro. Then the Nation of Islam, the present followers, like the Jews in the Bible, will be judged according to whether they will accept this new teaching that Allah is real and is and has been among us. When Allah raises His Prophet, this puts both on the scene at the same time, therefore, nothing can follow the prophet's teachings but heaven for the acceptors and chastisement for the rejectors - Judgment. Read how the Mahdi is raised from among our people by Allah, and how judgment follows his message. Mr. Muhammad Speaks article, "FOR WHEREVER THE CARCASS IS, THERE WILL THE EAGLES BE GATHERED TOGETHER." It says, "Take a look at Allah's servant (Abdul, the name Elijah would not take, see foot-note #6) in the Bible, it says, "Who was more blind, deaf and dumb as my Messenger whom I sent?" He is appointed by Allah God, and Allah has given Him the sheep (the Nation of Islam) to feed with the bread of truth (reality of Allah) and He will not give them to anyone else. Many will reject the Mahdi and will charge Him with not teaching what Mr. Muhammad has taught. Read in the same article, it says, "Many of the eagles (robbers, which include the weak Muslims here in America) have nothing to offer but arguments against the Shepherd (Mahdi) telling the sheep (followers of the Nation of Islam) that he the Shepherd is not the Messenger of Allah and that he is not an Apostle. The same article says, "No prophet of the past brought forth judgment unto truth, judgment for truths sake, comes at the end of the world. Jesus and Muhammad both failed to convert the Jews and Christians, but the last Messenger will not make an attempt to convert them. His teachings are to close the door against the enemies of Allah God and His Prophet. Judgment follows his message, for God is left to act after him. He is the end of the prophets because there is nothing left for a prophet to do after God has manifested Himself to the world, along with the last Messenger." Read the article "ISLAM MEANS UNITY", June 10, 1967. It says Messengers are never sent. They are always raised in the midst of those whom Allah would warn; so, they cannot claim that they did not understand the language of the Messenger or say that He was a foreigner or stranger. The Messenger is one from among them.

Chapter Two
WHO IS THE MESSENGER?

Foot-note #11 (Matt. 22:42)

This statement can be found on page 19 of Message To The Blackman. The author met the Saviour a few weeks after his baptism, or conversion to the faith. At that time Mr. Muhammad had been teaching 27 years, that the Son of Man was coming and would bring about a great change. The Saviour began to teach that we are all Gods, and that we should refer to each other as Lord, and that Allah was our Father, the wisest and Greatest of us all. This caused brothers and sisters (Jews) in Newark (Jerusalem) to reject him, saying his teaching is wrong and was not the same as Mr. Muhammad's. The Saviour began teaching the history of Noah and explaining that those who Noah saved were taken out of the midst of those he was sent to save. He called them his family. He did not come to save the world or everybody in it. He wants only those who accept Him and His Father Allah, Who sent Him to search for the Lost Sheep of the Holy Tribe of Shabazz. Everyone in the Nation of the old world of Islam (Jews) are not Shabazzians, nor are they Negroes. But God's Family is lost in the midst of these people. Therefore, God prepared a body, the Son of Man to come search for the lost sheep. Read the same above page 19. It says, "You have, heard of old that God prepared a body, or the expected Son of Man; Jesus is a specially prepared man to do a work of redeeming the Lost Sheep (the so-called Negro)." It is interesting to note that the body of the Son of Man had to be of two worlds. He would be born in the old world and would build a New World. He is able to go in and around the old world without the enemy discovering who He is, while He searches for the lost members of the family of God. Every brother and sister in the old world see and recognize Mr. Fard of 1930, so he would not be able to work in disguise. Not in this day and time. But the True Son of Man, today can travel all over the country undiscovered. The same article says, "This He has done in the person of Master W.F. Muhammad, the man who was made by His Father to go and search for the lost members of the Tribe of Shabazz. Master W.F. Muhammad is that Son of Man whom the world has been expecting to come for 2,000 years, seeking to save that which was lost." Page 19, "These are the days of the resurrection of the mentally dead, so-called Negroes. The Son of Man is here. His coming has been fulfilled. He seeks that which was lost (the so-called Negroes). Many now are receiving His name, and that name alone will save you. The wicked nations of the earth are sorry and angry to see the Son of Man set up a government of justice and peace over this, their wicked world." Same page, "We must have a new ruler and a new government, where the people can enjoy freedom, justice, and equality. Let the so-called Negroes rejoice, for Allah has prepared for them what the eye has not seen, the ear has not heard, and the heart has not been able to conceive." Fard Saviour, is now establishing this government, or (House of His Father's desire). Matt. 22:42 to 45.

Foot-note #12

This statement comes from the article Muhammad Speaks, "THE GREAT FALSEHOOD." The second coming of Jesus, means that a man who will fulfill the scriptures concerning Jesus, as it is written in the Bible prophecy, will show up at the end of the devil's time. The man who is with us today, the Mahdi, is the manifestation of the second coming of Jesus. Jesus of two thousand years ago, brought a book telling what would happen when Jesus (Justice) would come at the end of the world. The Bible is talking of Jesus of today, not of 2,000 years ago. Jesus of 2,000 years ago never was killed on the cross. This is all signs and symbols of the rejection and persecution of the Mahdi and His disciples today. Jesus of the past never had any disciples, he was killed before he could raise any followers. Some people believe that Master Fard Muhammad, of 1930, fulfilled the second coming of Jesus. That is the great misunderstanding. If Mr. Fard of 1930, fulfilled the second coming of Jesus in 1930, and we have been waiting for him to come again today, then this would be the third coming of Jesus. Mr. Fard of 1930 did not fulfill Jesus's second coming. The Saviour has just been born in our midst, and he is the Jesus we have been taught by God to wait for. This is the Jesus who will set us in heaven, and destroy our enemies.

Read THE GREAT FALSEHOOD, it says, "This is the Jesus of the second coming, a man with the same ideas that Jesus had concerning the infidels, that they should be destroyed and removed from the face of the earth, for there is no good in them." Fard Saviour, who is now in person among us, was crucified (mentally) by the Muslim Officials (Jews) of the old world of Islam. Fard Saviour's disciples were persecuted and run from the Mosque in Jerusalem (Newark). Fard Saviour bears witness to Elijah Muhammad, and Elijah bears witness to Fard Saviour, but the people in the Mosque rebelled. This is the exact history as it is prophesied in the Bible. John the Baptist did not deceive the people as to who and where the Saviour was to come. The people themselves paid little or no heed to what Elijah taught so they deceived themselves about Allah and His Last and Greatest Prophet, the Mahdi. (Read foot-note #2 chapter 1.)

Foot-note #13

This statement comes from the article "IN THIS WORLD OF CRISIS AND DESTRUCTION OF NATIONS, THE ONLY ESCAPE YOU HAVE IS IN ALLAH AND FOLLOWING HIS MESSENGER". March 4, 1967. This is a plain statement. God means power and force. Saviour means, one who saves or helps, also it is a title of Christ. Jesus is Allah's helper or Saviour. Jesus is the God, or the power and force by which we will enter the Kingdom of Heaven. We cannot enter except by or through Him. So Fard is our God, and Elijah's Saviour. Read Psalms 110:1 "The Lord said unto my Lord, sit thou on my right hand until I make thine enemies thy footstool."

Foot-note #14

This statement comes from the article Mr. Muhammad Speaks "JESUS PRAYS FOR HIS DISCIPLES", JULY 15, 1966. Jesus is the Great Mahdi, the Messiah. The man who authorized Him to teach is His Father, Allah in Person. Fard Saviour teaches the truth that has been kept secret for millions of years. The author bears witness that Fard is the first begotten of the dead. No one knew the person of Almighty God Allah, until Mr. Fard Saviour was commissioned Field Minister of the Nation of Islam, February 26, 1960. The old world would not accept this great man from the beginning. Fard Saviour fulfilled the prophecy of Jesus by raising his disciples (staff) in the field. It should be obvious that the Great Angel, Fard of 1930, did not raise twelve disciples and teach them the secret of Allah being God among us. Elijah, was the only one who knew the whole truth, and He would not tell it until after 12 years after Fard had left, 1946. It is this Saviour, born in our midst, who is saying to His Father, Allah, to bless the true believers whom He has taught the reality of his presence among us, and who have accepted His authority. Read St. John 17:25-26. "O righteous

Father, the world hath not known thee, and these have known that thou hast sent me. And I have delivered unto them Thy name, and will declare it; that this love where with Thou hast loved me may be in them, and I in them." Also read 1 to 4 of the same chapter, it says, "These words spoke Jesus and lifted up his eyes to heaven, and said, Father, the hour is come; glorify thy Son, that thy Son also may glorify Thee." (Here the hour stands for the time for the promise of Allah to come into reality, heaven for Jesus and His followers.) "As Thou hast given him power over all flesh, that he should give eternal life to as many as thou hast given him. And this is life eternal, that they might know thee the only true God, and Jesus Christ, whom thou hast sent. I have glorified thee on the earth: I have finished the work which thou gavest me to do."

Now that Fard Saviour, has restored the true knowledge of Allah, on earth by teaching His disciples, His work is done, but He prays to Allah to bless His disciples, because their work has just begun. The Kingdom will be built by the work of their own hands, under the direction of the Holy Ghost. Read Holy Qur'an 2:87, "And we indeed gave Moses the book, and we sent Messengers after him one after the other; and we gave Jesus, son of Mary, clear arguments and strengthened him with the Holy Spirit." Read St. John 14:17, "Even the Spirit of truth; whom the world cannot receive, because it seeth him not, neither knoweth him: but ye know him; for he dwelleth with you, and shall be in you." 15:26, "But when the Comforter is come, whom I will send unto you from the Father, even the Spirit of truth, which proceedeth from the Father, he shall testify of me:" 16:14, "He shall glorify me: for he shall receive of mine, and shall show it unto you." This brother ghost is the Spokesman for the Prophet, Aaron, the keeper of the staff, Jesus's first disciple.

Foot-note #15

This statement comes from the article Muhammad Speaks "JESUS A SIGN AND EXAMPLE". The Most Hon. Mr. Elijah Muhammad makes the truth so plain in this article; I must quote the first paragraph. "Let me make myself clear to you in regard to last week's article. I am not trying to condemn the history of Jesus as being false; but rather I am trying to put the meaning and signs, or miracles where they belong. That is in the present so-called Negroes history and Jesus today. Jesus said his parents were only a sign or prototype of that which was to come. Of course, there are many student ministers in the theological college seminaries, who probably know, or are learning that most of what the Bible gives us of Jesus' history has got to be a future man and not one answering any such description of 2,000 years ago." Is it not clear that Fard Saviour is Jesus raised from among the so-called Negroes? Read the article JESUS WAS ONLY A PROPHET. Mr. Muhammad says, "The revelations of St. John 1:11, quote: "I am Alpha and Omega, the first and the last." They refer to Jesus saying this on his return from death. The same thing is being preached now, from the coming of Allah, in the person of Master Fard Muhammad." Again Mr. Muhammad not only makes it plain that Fard is among us, but He describes the opposition to His work of creating the New World and the years of His war with the old world of Islam here in America. Read the article "BREAKING UP OF A WHITE CIVILIZATION". "The disbelievers and hypocrites of my people also are angry over the change of the old world to a New World of justice and righteousness, causing much spiritual darkness and misunderstanding to fall upon them. They want to judge the person Allah should choose for His Messenger." This article was written February 26, 1966. It also says, "The day of decision between the dark races or nations was begun by God Himself in the person of Master Fard Muhammad, to whom be Praise Forever, as is prophesied in the Bible "Multitude in the valley of decision, for the day (before or by 1970) of the Lord is near in the valley of decision." (Joel 3:14). Also read, "THE TIME AND WHAT MUST BE DONE", June 16, 1967, where it says, "Jesus told them that he did not come to destroy the law of Moses, but to fulfill the law." He said to the Jews that Moses gave the law to them but none of them kept it. This is the day that shall prove these words of prophecy. Study the prophecies of both the Bible and the Holy Qur'an and you will learn that you are living in the days of the Judgment of the world." Mr. Muhammad taught the law and what must be done to the old world for 36 years, but none would do as he bid them. Now the Mahdi has come to establish the New World, by gathering the true believers out of the old world of Islam.

Read how the Messiah, Jesus, or the Mahdi, will build the New World in the article - "IN THE HEREAFTER, NO MEDICINE NO DRUGS." Mr. Muhammad says, "Note the beginning awakening of the Blackman is very swift. This is due to the fact that he once was a great original ruler. His scientists can set themselves in order under the guidance of that Mighty One who the world has been looking for to come and head the change over to the construction of a New World, with new laws and new rulers to govern the New World, making the progress fast, but with sure success." The same article states, "No pattern of the former world is allowed by a new God who has ideas and wisdom which is latent in him which, if given a chance, "Can Build Something Different." Also, the same article says, "But this New World which is prophesied of will put an end to temporary kingdoms, as the Holy Qur'an and the Bible refers to the Mahdi, or the Messiah (God) (in person) as being wiser than them all. He will build a civilization and government with infinite wisdom that will live forever. This is the world that is emerging in the old world. This is what we are being qualified for." Also, in the same article it says, "The teaching of what the people who are trying to qualify for the hereafter will be and do, begins with the coming of

Allah, (God) according to many prophecies of the Bible and hints found in the Holy Qur'an reading and studies." Read the book of Revelations in your Bible concerning the coming of the Great Kingdom of Allah and His Prophet Jesus Christ, The Lamb.

Foot-note #16

This statement comes from the book Message To The Blackman page 141. The above shows that Fard, Mahdi and the Christ are the same man. Read the same book page 137, it says, "In fact, if the Bible is rightly understood, it is referring to none other than the so-called Negroes and their enemies, the chosen people of God to whom the God gave the firstborn (convert), and even the (Mahdi) Christ offered His life to restore the so-called Negroes again to their own kind." Here Mr. Muhammad speaks of three people, God Allah, the Prophet Fard, and the Firstborn (convert) the disciples, all working together to save the so-called Negroes.

Foot-note #17

This statement comes from the article "THE 144,000". The Christ is here spoken of as being the symbolic Lamb, read St. John 1:29, "The next day John seeth Jesus coming unto him and saith behold! The Lamb of God, which taketh away the sin of the world." Verse 36 says, "And looking upon Jesus as he walked, he saith, Behold the Lamb of God!" February 24, 1960 the author met Fard Saviour in Chicago, for the Saviour's Day Convention. Fard had arrived with little or no money nor did he have a place to stay (hotel). Fard had complete faith that Allah would provide for Him, and Allah did. The Saviour ate with the author, and slept in the same bed with the author. Fard wanted to make a pallet on the floor of the room but the author convinced him that we all sleep on the floor if He did. So Fard, not wanting us on the floor shared the bed. Fard Saviour's blue suit was clean, but one look by a watchful eye would reveal that our

Beloved companion was poverty stricken. There was a patch over the right knee of his pants. At this time Mr. Fard Saviour really looked like the Lamb who was slain, mentally and economically. Nevertheless, it was on this very occasion, the 26th of February, that it was made known publicly that Mr. Fard Saviour was the Official Representative of the House of God, Mosque 25. He, Fard, was the only one who responded to the God's Call. (This call that God, Allah, made will be dealt with fully in foot-note #20).

No one else throughout the world of Islam could answer this call. Read Rev. 5:6 to 9, "And I beheld, and lo, in the midst of the throne and of the four beasts, and in the midst of the elders, stood a Lamb as it had been slain, having seven horns and seven eyes, which are the seven Spirits of God sent forth into all the earth. And he came and took the book out of the right hand of him that sat upon the throne. And when he had taken the book, the four beasts and four and twenty elders fell down before the Lamb, having every one of them harps, and golden vials full of odors, which are the prayers of saints. And they sung a new song, saying, Thou art worthy to take the book, and to open the seals thereof: for thou wast slain, and hast redeemed us to God by thy blood out of every kindred, and tongue, and people, and nation." The above makes it clear that Christ, called the Lamb, took the book from his Father's (Allah's) hand, and there after began to teach a doctrine called new, or a new song. Rev. 14: is a prophecy of the success of Master Fard, whose teachings are to bring man face to face with Allah. 14:1 says, "And I looked and lo, a Lamb stood on Mount Zion; and with him a 144,000 having his Father's name written in their foreheads." Mr. Fard gives His followers one of His Father's names, which are one of the 99 attributes of Allah. Also Mr. Fard's Fruit has a mark in their foreheads, produced by praying properly five times a day. Mr. Muhammad explains this mark in this article, "THE 144,000". Read where he says a special mark will distinguish the righteous from the devils and it will be in their heads (foreheads) caused by prostrating. The mark according to the Holy Qur'an that will be in their foreheads - will be from prostrating. The Muslims prostrate in their prayers on rough floors or rugs, which produces a mark on their foreheads. Some of my followers have such a sign now, produced by 5 prayers a day obligation." Let us read what the Holy Qur'an says about this subject. Chapter 48: Section 4, "Ultimate Triumph of Islam": "Allah indeed fulfilled the vision for His Messenger with truth. You shall certainly enter the Sacred Mosque, if Allah please, in security, your heads shaved and hair cut short, not fearing. But He knows what you know not, so He has ordained a near victory before that. He it is Who has sent His Messenger with the guidance and the religion of Truth that He may make it prevail over all religions. And Allah is enough for a witness. Muhammad is the Messenger of Allah, and those with him are firm of heart against the disbelievers, compassionate among themselves. Thou seest them bowing down, prostrating themselves, seeking Allah's grace and pleasure. Their marks are on their faces in consequence of prostration. That is their description in the Torah - and their description in the Gospel - like seed produce that puts forth its sprout, then strengthens it, so it becomes stout and stands firmly on its stem, delighting the sowers that He may enrage the disbelievers on account of them. Allah has promised such of them as believe and do good, forgiveness and a great reward." (End of Qur'an section 4 quote.) Who is this Muhammad? Is it the one of the past or the one of the future? For sure it is the Future Muhammad, that is spoken of in the great prophecy! Read what Mr. Muhammad says in the Book Message To The Blackman page 159. It says, "If you study the prophecy concerning the last Messenger of God, according to the description given to the man by the Bible's prophecy in the Torah and Gospel, you will find that he is a man, according to the Psalms, with the name of "Muhammad" and also you will find him in the

Revelations under the symbolical name, "Lamb," He gets the name (Praised) from the honor of the "twenty-four elders" or Islamic Scientists. The position that he is shown under, the symbolical "Lamb" in Revelations, is like the Holy Qur'an's teaching one who is illiterate and whom the people will find written down in the Torah and the Gospel. (The book of Isaiah; the parables of Jesus). This is the man the above prayer is made for because he, as one of the Islamic writers says, will be born among the infidels. The revelations of the Bible symbolically place him in the midst of "four-beasts." Therefore, prayer must be made for his protection among a people without the teachings of Islam - not a country where never had any former prophets of Allah risen and set up signs of the future greatness of Islam, as had Arabia in the time of Muhammad. The signs of the future of Islam and its last Messenger, Abraham, had already been set up in the Holy City Mecca. Muhammad did not destroy these signs, but rather he repaired the sign to live until it had served its purpose."

Foot-note #18

This statement is from the article "MISINTERPRETATION AND MISUNDERSTANDING", also page 188 in Message To The Blackman. The Holy Qur'an is a true book. It predicts the last prophet, Muhammad, and His God, Allah, at the time of judgment. From cover to the back of this great book speaks of judgment of the world. Muhammad of 1,400 years ago did not bring about the judgment of the world. Read where the above article says, "Many of the Orthodox Muslims do not want to believe that Allah has appeared in the Person of Master Fard Muhammad or that He has made manifest the truth that has been hidden from their religious scientists-the truth of God and of the devil as revealed to me. Though they do have the Holy Qur'an, many of them do not understand the meaning of it, and some of them believe everything that is prophesied in the Bible and Holy Qur'an about a last Messenger or Prophet being or referring to Muhammad of 1,400 years ago. They even take all of the people prophesied from Moses to Jesus, who received a prophet coming after Moses and like Moses to the people of Muhammad of 1,400 years ago. This is very wrong. It must be understood that the prophesies are referring to God and a Messenger in the resurrection of the dead in the last years of this world ruled by the Caucasian people." "Both of you, Christians and Orthodox Muslims, are absolutely wrong to believe all of this prophecy refers to Jesus or Moses and a prophet like himself and to believe that the symbolic lamb in Revelations refers to Jesus or, as the Orthodox Muslims believe, that it refers to Muhammad of 1,400 years ago. How gravely you must interpret your Bible and Holy Qur'an. This important understanding is causing a lot of division." The same article says, "The Holy Qur'an refers to the days of Allah, meaning in the years of the resurrection, and it often repeats that the people will meet with Allah in person, not in visions." The Muslims in the East believe Allah is a spirit. This same article further says, "There are some religious scientists in Islam who know these things to be true that I am saying, and there are those who do not understand their Holy Qur'an and the prophecy of Muhammad being lost among the dead, for the Bible teaches that God will use him to make Himself known in the last days." Same article says, "The so-called Negro must be delivered by God and God only. He will use a Messenger who is symbolically referred to as the Lamb of God in the Resurrection to spiritually liberate the American Negro." You should also read the article "THE BATTLE IN THE SKY" page 293 in the book Message To The Blackman. It shows the prophecy of the Lamb at the end of the world of the devils. It says, "Allah, whom we praise, comes in the Person of Master W. F. Muhammad, the Great Mahdi, expected by the Muslims, and the anti-Christs (the devils) under the names: Son of Man, Jesus Christ, Messiah, God,

Lord, Jehovah, the Last (Jehovah) and the Christ. These meanings are good and befitting as titles, but the meaning of His name 'Mahdi', as mentioned in the Holy Qur'an Sharrieff 22:54, is better. All of these names refer to Him. His name, Fard Muhammad, is beautiful in its meaning. He must bring an end to war, and the only way to end war between man and man is to destroy the war-maker (the trouble maker)." There are several articles of the judgment of this world and the battle in the sky, in the book Message To The Blackman. You should study them. Master Fard Muhammad taught me about this sky battle, and how it would come about. Master Fard Muhammad taught me that the woman of Revelations 12, in the Bible, refers to him (the Christ) and that the Child she gave birth to, is his disciples, who was to rule the nations, but the devil was fighting to prevent the Child from establishing themselves in the land. But Allah provides for the woman and protects the child from the devil until the child is grown enough to enter the Sacred Mosque.

(Read Holy Qur'an foot-note #17). This is the first victory. After the Lamb and his followers have escaped the evil plans of the devils and are rulers of the Sacred Mosque and the city in which it is, much praise will be sung of the Holy One. The City will be called the Camp of the Saints. Read page 185 of Message To The Blackman. Mr. Muhammad said, Revelations states that the Lamb and his followers, after escaping the evil plans of the beast, sang the song of Moses, which was the victory over Pharaoh. Master Fard Muhammad taught me that this victory of Moses that the Lamb sang is the opening of the fulfillment of Moses history, as it is prophesied in the Bible and Holy Qur'an. (Moses history is dealt with in foot-note #19.) The Saviour taught me that the devil will become so angry because of our success throughout the country, he will (the devil) make one last attempt to destroy the Holy City, and His disciples. The devil will bring his army and surround the city, (St. Luke 21:20), at this time no food will come in or out, the water will be cut off.

This is why Master Fard, says we will have to stay in the habit of fasting; also why we must save beans and water. Master Fard Muhammad, taught me that this great attack on us by the devil's army, will bring Allah to our aid. Allah will do battle for us to show the world that Allah is with us and that He is the most powerful God in the Universe. Master Fard, said this battle will take place in the sky. It is at this time the devil will give us independence on some of this land, and offer to support us for 25 years. This is the complete fulfillment of all prophecies of Jesus, Muhammad, Moses, the Lamb and Mahdi, of today, born among us. Not those of the past. Read what Mr. Muhammad says in the article, "THE FULFILLMENT OF PROPHECIES SEEN", page 285 in Message To The Blackman, where it says, "Many will come saying that they are the Christ but none of these false prophets can do the job of fulfilling the scriptures and raising the dead. Even to the late Maulana Muhammad Ali, who also claimed himself to have been Christ, the Messiah, when he was among the Christians, the Jews, Hindu, and among the Muslims, their Mahdi." Only Allah and His Messenger, the Great Mahdi, have the power to raise the dead. (Read Message to the Blackman page 118, actual history of Moses.)

Foot-note #19

This statement comes from the article, "PLAN TO DESTROY OUR RACE" page 67 in Message To The Blackman. The history of Moses as written in the Bible refers to the last Prophet, the Great Mahdi. We have two histories of Moses as Master Fard Muhammad taught me. One is the actual life of the prophet who was a half original man and was sent to the caves of Europe to raise the devils 4,000 years ago, this is Moses of the past. Second, we have the prophecy of Moses who fights and wins independence for his people who would be slaves to a most powerful government: this is a Future Moses, the Last Messenger of Allah. Read Message To The

Blackman page 157, it says, "The Orthodox Muslims thinks this refers to Arabia and that Muhammad (may the peace and blessings of Allah be upon Him and may He forever be one with Allah) of nearly 1,400 years ago was the one fulfilling the answer to Abraham's prayers. But if they look at it again and ponder over it, it is like their belief in thinking that Muhammad of nearly 1,400 years ago was a prophet like Moses, that Moses prophesied in Deut. 18:18. But they forget that Moses was a man who was raised in the house of bondage under a king who held him and his people in bondage to him and to his false worship of God and religion. And he desired no one to interfere with his teachings, given to his slaves. His fear, according to the Holy Qur'an, was that Moses would change the religion. The Orthodox Muslims think this was fulfilled in the Meccans' opposition to Muhammad. Not so! He does not compare with the prophecy of a man like Moses, for there was no king singled out who opposed Muhammad in Mecca. There was no separation of the Arabs from any slave-masters and a destruction of the slave-masters. It was a certain class of people of science."

You must also understand that Mr. Fard of 1930 (peace and blessings of Allah be upon Him) did not win independence on some of this land for us. Mr. Fard did not bring His brother with Him. Moses comes with His brother who is Moses' Spokesman, Aaron. Nor did Fard of 1930, ever go to Pharaoh (Washington D.C.) to ask for our independence. This all happens with the coming of the Lamb. Read the prophecy of the two prophets in the Bible, Rev. 11: also, read the Holy Qur'an 26:10-11, it says, "And when the Lord called Moses, saying; Go to the iniquitous people - The people of Pharaoh. Will they not guard against evil?" Also read Holy Qur'an 28:35 "He said: We will strengthen thine arm with thy brother, and We will give you both an authority, so that they shall not reach you. With Our signs, you two and those who follow you, will triumph." Also read Exodus 4: of how Moses and His brother Aaron are called and sent to Pharaoh. Read what it says in Message To The Blackman page 155. "The Bible shows (Exodus 16:2,3,8) that it was the want of bread and meat first of all that gave Moses and Aaron much trouble trying to lead the people into the spiritual knowledge of Jehovah and self-independence. They even said when they were hungry: "Would to God we had died by the hand of the Lord in the land of Egypt (Exodus 16:3). Oftentimes, they angered Moses and Aaron by their longing for the food of their slave masters even while on their way to freedom and self-independence." Master Fard Muhammad has taught me that after the victory of the Lamb, (which means after we have labored in the field until we have enough followers who believe as we believe, then our God Allah, will give us His Sacred House, as well as authority over all other - openly and publicly - Mosques in the Nation of Islam), we will start fulfilling the history of Moses. Some of our people in the Nation of Islam will rebel and give trouble to Moses and Aaron, questioning their authority. Read page 28 Message To The Blackman, it says, "It took the destruction of the people of Korah by Almighty God to make Israel understand that it was God who had appointed Moses to lead them and that self-made leaders such as Korah would not work in the way of delivering Israel to another country. Because Allah had chosen Moses to act as a guide for Israel, and all other self-made leaders would be failures."

Master Fard taught me that there will be a year chastisement for all the rebels in the Nation who refuse to accept His (Fard's) authority; and He (Fard) will send His staff against them. Master Fard Muhammad taught me that this will bring about a separation of the true believers and the hypocrites. Read Message To The Blackman page 28. It says, "He sent poisonous and fiery serpents against them to bite and kill those who rebelled. So, this is a warning and a sign for us today; That when God intends to separate a people, or remove a people and put another in their stead, it is His work and the people who rebel against His work will come to naught." Master Fard Muhammad taught me that our national activity of exposing the devil as the universal enemy, will make the government of America angry, and they will accuse us of changing the religion of the so-called Negroes. They will falsely charge us with subversive action against the government. This, Master Fard taught me, is why Moses will be called to the capital. The House Un-American Activities Committee, will send for Moses and Aaron to affirm or deny the false charges made against them, but Moses will ignore such false charges and demand that we be given independence on some of this land that we can call our own. Let my people go! This Pharaoh (white slavemaster) will not do, until Allah whips him into submission with the forces of nature and finally the battle in the sky. The result of this battle will be our independence on some of this land, (the promised land). All nations will bear witness that Allah is God and is among us. America will support us for twenty years. We will give the people the choice of coming into our state; of which the borders will be protected by passports and visas, or stay with the American white people. However, most of our people will come with us into our land. But that is not the complete end of America, it is when we win independence that our people will come. Read Message To The Blackman page 46, it says, "It is written (Rev. 14:1) that 144,000 of us will accept and return to our God and people and the rest of my people will go down with the enemies of Allah. For this sad prophecy of the loss of my people I write what I am writing, hoping perhaps that you may be able to beat the old prophets' predictions by making the truth so simple that a fool can understand it." Master Fard Muhammad taught me that most of our people will come with us into our state and will enjoy heaven for 20 to 25 years, but 97% will refuse to leave this country when it is time to go back to Egypt.

Today the old world officials are opposed to Moses and his

brother Aaron, who are bringing about this change of worlds under the guidance of Almighty Allah. But the opposition will be the loser. Read Message To The Blackman page 50, "WE MUST TEACH OUR OWN", it says, "The Orthodox Muslims will have to bow to the choice of Allah. Allah will bring about a New Islam. As for the Principles of Belief, they remain the same. There will be no more signs to be watched for the coming of God and the setting up of a New World of Islam. We are seeing this change now and entering into it. The devils oppose this change, and the Orthodox join them in opposing us because of their desire to carry on the old way of Islam. Allah will place those of His choice in authority in the making of the New World, and others must obey whomever He places in authority or find themselves fighting against the power of whomever they hold to be on their side and in their favor. We must have a New World. We accept for a New Nation completely.

As Yakub brought about a new people (the present white race) who were a completely new people made out of the original of us, another new people must be made to be the ruling voice of tomorrow out of this old world that is now living her last days. They will be completely new people. The Holy Qur'an and Bible refer to them as being brought about by the power and will of God in Person in the resurrection of the mentally dead, lost-found original people in America. We may not seem to please you or to be pleasing to Allah, but it is written in the Bible that He will give to whom He pleases and chastise whom He pleases. This is to warn us that we have no choice in the matter. Whatever Allah desires, He will bring into being, whether we like it or not." Moses and Aaron and the staff are now among us but few know it.

Foot-note #20

This statement was made by Mr. Elijah Muhammad, December 1959, while on his way to Mecca. Mr. Muhammad paid a surprise visit at New York Mosque No. 7. Master Fard Muhammad was in the county jail and I (the author) had just been released on bail from the same county jail. The devil had falsely charged Fard Saviour and myself with violating his (the devils) laws. However, the author was present at this surprise meeting. It was at this time that the above statement was made, also at the same time Fard Saviour, received his revelation of coming into the prison and raising the new ministers. When Fard Saviour was released from jail He made His intentions known and was commissioned Official Representative of the Model Mosque. That February 26, 1960, he was commissioned National Field Minister and was put in charge of all Muslims wherever he might go. The author was a witness to this. The surprise meeting was as always beautiful - and the Saviour's Day Convention February 26, 1960 will always be remembered by the author. It is only fitting to give some statements from both these important meetings. Here are some statements made before going to Mecca: "Stop worrying about a job, work for Allah." "I can give you to Allah now." "I will continue to teach you until Allah tells me job well done, and I think I will still whisper." "Ask Allah for what you want, try Him, Allah will answer your prayers." "If you ask Allah to dry up the Atlantic Ocean He will do it for you, not that I am telling you to ask for such a thing, but I am saying that Allah will answer your prayers."

When Mr. Elijah Muhammad came back from Mecca and spoke at the Saviours' Day meeting, He said, "The executioners are on the way." "When it gets too hot for me, it's just right for the Mahdi, and the temperature now is 212° degrees." "I am in favor of putting our women back into the veils." The author has heard rumor that Mr. Muhammad, while Mr. Muhammad was in Mecca the wise men (scientists) asked him many questions about Islam and he answered them all. Then He asked them all one question and none of them could answer it. Then Mr. Muhammad told them that if He would have known that He would have to teach the students He would have come prepared. It is also said that Mr. Muhammad said that He could see the pages of the Holy Qur'an turning over in their heads, trying to find an answer to His question. I have heard that the question Mr. Muhammad asked was, "Who Is The Original Man?" The above story reminds me of the disciples and the old world officials. The disciples must teach the old world their own lessons, and books.

If we would ask the old world, *Who is the Original Man,* they would say everything but Allah - they don't know Allah or His Prophet - or His disciples. We are prepared to teach the truth to the old world, but our teaching will separate the sheep from the goats. Many of our people are held in subjection by the old world officials, who are ignorant of Allah and His plan to resurrect our people. We have waited a very long time for this day, now it will be taught that Allah is in person among us, along with His Prophet, Master Fard Muhammad. The New World is born. This truth will never be hid again. Our government's foundation is built upon truth: we will make as much progress - as we teach. If we don't teach this truth we will not be established in the land, and Allah will remove us, and raise disciples who will obey His order to teach. No one other than Allah, the Prophet, and the Angels are aware of this Divine Supreme Knowledge. Everyone is waiting on us. The whole world knows that this is the time of the hidden truth to be revealed. And we are the blessed ones to have been the first to receive it. There is no knowledge greater than the knowledge of the person of Almighty God Allah. Therefore, there is no man greater on this earth in wisdom and true knowledge and of understanding, than Master Fard Muhammad, and His disciples. Now we must teach. So you must study, so that you may raise the dead by the thousands. This is the time of the great resurrection and this little book bears witness that the Angel Gabriel, is blowing his horn, (a symbol of power as in the Bible - horn of salvation). We are the help of Allah, who will build the House of our Father's Desire with the guidance of His Prophet, Master Fard Muhammad. Teach Islam and heaven will be ours forever.

Remember that the Moorish Americans opposed Elijah just as the old world is opposing us. The Moorish Americans accepted W. D. Fard, but they rejected Elijah, even though they knew Elijah was the favorite of Fard. Mr. Muhammad had to teach a new teaching, just as the Mahdi and His disciples today must do. These so-called followers of W. D. Fard, (the Moorish Americans) had their headquarters in Newark, N.J. Elijah was run out of this city by these people who thought that they believed in Islam. They also thought that they knew the true identity of W. D. Fard, but no one but Elijah Muhammad knew that secret and He would not tell it until 12 years had passed. During this time Mr. Muhammad would not say that He was the Messenger of Allah. He was known as the Supreme Minister. This is the same thing that is happening today. Fard Saviour is known as the Field Minister, and His true identity is unknown to the old world, who think they are scientist in Islam. They know not what they believe. W. D. Fard taught thousands, but Elijah had to raise his own followers in the field and in prison. No one gave Elijah anything, he had to go for himself as the Great Mahdi must go for Himself. We are the first Ministers of the Great Mahdi, therefore, no one is going to teach and raise fruit for us. The Mahdi had only Allah with Him when He raised us, His disciples. We cannot look for any help other than Allah and His prophets in teaching and raising the dead.

Chapter Three
WHO ARE THE DISCIPLES?

Foot-note #21 (Matt. 16:13 - Mark 8:27 - Luke 8:18)

This statement comes from the article, "THE GREAT FALSEHOOD" March 11, 1967. It should be understood by now that Jesus's history as it is found in the Holy Qur'an and the Bible - are prophecies of today. Therefore, all pictures or scriptures of any kind of him and his disciples are false. Jesus and his disciples are in our midst today and no one except Allah, outside of Jesus and his followers know the true identity of Jesus and his disciples. Jesus told his disciples to keep their identity a secret until the Comforter came.

He, Jesus, had to come as a thief in the night, as it is written in the prophecy Rev. 16:15, "Behold, I come as a thief. Blessed is he that watcheth, and keepeth his garments, lest he walk naked, and they see his shame." In the Nation of Islam here in America, today there is much talk about Fard Saviour. Some say He is a self-made prophet, some say He is Elijah's successor. But Fard would not let it be known that He was the Saviour. (Read Matt. 16:13-21) "When Jesus came unto the coasts of Caesarea Philippi, he asked his disciples, saying, Whom do men say that I, the Son of Man, am? And they said, some say that thou art John the Baptist; some, Elias; and others, Jeremiahs, or one of the prophets. He saith unto them, But whom say ye that I am? And Simon Peter answered and said, Thou art the Christ, the Son of the living God. And Jesus answered and said unto him, Blessed art thou, Simon Barjona: for flesh and blood hath not revealed it unto thee, but my father which is in heaven. And I say also unto thee, That thou art Peter, and upon this rock I will build my church; and the gates of hell shall not prevail against it. And I will give unto thee the keys of the Kingdom of heaven: and whatsoever thou shalt bind on earth shall be bound in heaven; and whatsoever thou shalt loose on earth shall be loosed in heaven. Then charged he his disciples that they should tell no man that he was Jesus the Christ. From that time forth began Jesus to show unto his disciples, how that he must go unto Jerusalem, and suffer many things of the elders and chief priests and scribes, and be killed, and be raised again the third day." (1966-1967-1968, three days.) Jesus taught the above to His disciples, but some forgot what Jesus said. The old world, being blind to the true knowledge of God, Allah, and His Prophet, opposed Master Fard and persecuted Him just as the prophecy says, Jesus's followers were separated from John the Baptist's followers, just as the field agent is separated from the Mosque, even though John loves Jesus, and Elijah loves us, there had to be a separation from the old world and the New World. The same thing took place with Abraham, and his nephew Lot. Lot received his divine authority from Abraham, and Abraham loved Lot and Lot loved Abraham, but their followers had to be separated. Read Genesis 13:7, "And there was strife between the herdmen of Abraham's cattle and the herdmen of Lot's cattle." There must be a separation of the old world from the New World. Jesus said, don't put new wine in old bottles. The old world does not know that they are still mentally dead, they think they are saved.

Jesus told His disciples that they would have to wait 3 years until He had gone through all the persecution and rejection at the hands of the old world, before the disciples can realize the heaven, or New World that Jesus had promised them. Matt. 24:13, "But he that shall endure until the end, the same shall be saved." The next verse of the same chapter 24:14, is referring to the end of the power of the old world to suppress the truth of the New World. It says, "And this Gospel of the Kingdom shall be preached in all the world for a witness unto all nations." Jesus told the disciples that after He fulfills the prophecy He would leave them, but they would have the Comforter with them to fulfill all that Jesus had promised them. Now the time has come to teach the glorification of Allah and His Prophet. Read how Peter began to teach after Jesus had fulfilled His mission. Acts 2:32 to 33, it says, "This Jesus hath God raised up, whereof we all are witnesses". Therefore, being by the right hand of God exalted, and having received of the Father, the promise of the Holy Ghost is Peter, who was commissioned by Jesus to take charge of His disciples and teach, for the time had come for their teachings to bring about the New World. Read St. John 21:15, it says, "So when they dined, Jesus saith to Simon Peter, Simon, son of Jonas, lovest thou me more than these? He saith unto him, Yea, Lord; thou knowest that I love thee. He saith unto him, Feed my lambs." Thus it is Peter who starts the new teaching to be known and Jesus informs His disciples, that all wishing to enter heaven or the New World would have to accept Peter and his authority. Read Matt. 12:32, it says, "And whosoever speaketh a word against the Son of Man, it shall be forgiven him: but whosoever speaketh against the Holy Ghost, it shall not be forgiven him, neither in this world, neither in the world to come." Peter is Jesus's first Fruit and does what Jesus tells him to do, so if you reject one you reject the other. Read Acts 1:2. "Until the day in which he was taken up, after that he through the Holy Ghost had given commandments unto the apostles whom he had chosen." Read these first chapters of Acts, and see the prophecy of the New World's beginning. See how this new truth will make wise men out of babies (youth 16 to 30). Also read the opposition of the old world to this great change, in the article from The Muhammad Speaks ("AMERICA HASTENS OWN DOOM") it shows how at the time when we begin to teach the truth (resurrection of the dead) the old world officials will try to stop the teaching, but will fail, because falsehood cannot overcome the truth. Their opposition to us is the opposition to Allah and His prophet, the Great Mahdi. Read the above article where it says, "We are in a world that is passing out of existence, and she is putting up a fight (war) to destroy the nation of righteousness. Beware! To try to oppose the success of Allah's truth, only hastens the doom of falsehood and teachers." The same article says, "Falsehood cannot be victorious over truth, as it triumphs over falsehood."

It should be clear to you that the first resurrection was Jesus and His disciples. We must now start resurrecting the people by teaching the whole truth under the direction of the Holy Ghost. The same article says, "Their ultimate aim is to do as their people always have done - try to destroy the preacher of truth and those who believe and follow him. This was the aim of Cain when he slew his brother Abel, and the aim of the dragon when he sought to destroy the woman (the Messenger) as it is written in Revelation 12:4." Cain represents the old world officials, who, because of their envy of Fard Saviour, killed Him mentally. Cain was angry because Allah loved Abel and accepted Abel's gifts, because Abel would only bring the best of what He had as a present for Allah. But Cain would only offer Allah what he (Cain) didn't want himself. So, the Lord would not accept anything from Cain. Cain thought by killing his brother Abel, he would get the favors of the Lord (Allah). But this deed of Cain only brought Allah's chastisement on Cain, and honor forever for Abel. Read what Mr. Muhammad says about the struggle we are now facing with the old world who do not want us to teach, (what is in this little book). In the article, "THE RESURRECTION OF OUR PEOPLE", page 278 (Message to the Blackman), Mr. Muhammad said, "The old world must be removed to make way for the New World. There is a universal struggle being waged by the old world against the beginning of the New World. Will the old world's opposition prevent the establishment of the New World? According to recorded history the efforts being made by the old world against the beginning of a New World will fail, as did former opponents of Allah." The same article says, "According to the Bible and Holy Qur'an, He (Messenger) was called a liar and looked upon as a crazy person."

Even though we have this opposition, this truth must be told, if it cost our lives. Allah is our protector and we will be successful. This truth of Allah and His Prophet Master Fard Muhammad, as taught by us, the disciples (Ministers of the Lord) will bring about the long awaited resurrection of our people, causing many to come over to us in companies in Jerusalem. We are to start in this city as it is prophesied in the Bible, St. Luke 24:46-47, it says, "And said unto them, Thus it is written, and thus it behooved Christ to suffer, and to rise from the dead the third day. And that repentance and remission of sins should be preached in his name among all nations, beginning at Jerusalem." Also read Acts 1:8, "But ye shall receive power, after that the Holy Ghost is come upon you: and ye shall be witnesses unto me both in Jerusalem, and in all Judea, and in Samaria, and unto the uttermost part of the earth." This prophecy shows that our teachings will not be short lived, it will not stop in Jerusalem, it will spread throughout the nation in a very small space of time. Before long, the whole world will be making arrangements to send people to learn our doctrine: some kings and queens will come themselves.

We are the people - the only people who know all the truth - and no one else will know this truth except through us. Read the article "ACCEPT YOUR OWN", August 8, 1964, it says, "Allah is handling the affair in person in the name of Master Fard Muhammad. He has chosen us today to be His people and mean to take us and build and establish forever, a people of righteousness and a people with unlimited knowledge of the Divine Supreme

Being. The very least one of these will be greater than the greatest of this world." This is only talking about Jesus and His disciples of today and their work of resurrecting the dead.

Foot-note #22

This statement can be found on page 186 in Message To The Blackman. The religious scientists referred to here, are the disciples who know that Allah is in person among us, and that Muhammad, the Great Mahdi, is the last and Greatest Messenger.

Foot-note #23

This statement can be found in the article, "THE MAKING OF THE DEVIL" page 108. We are the scientists of Islam now, and was the scientists whenever the writing of history took place. It is our job to write it and then see to it that everyone lives it. We have 9,046 years to this 25,000 years of history to live before we write again.

Foot-note #24

This statement can be found on page 158 in Message To The Blackman. We do honor the Lamb - when we know who He is. The scientists are the first to recognize Him. Read Rev. 15:3, "And they sing the song of Moses the servant of God, and the song of the Lamb, saying, Great and marvelous are thy works, Lord God Almighty; just and true are thy ways, thou King of Saints."

Foot-note #25

This statement was made by Mr. Muhammad, 1960 - February 26, Saviour's Day Convention. The executioners are none other than the Fruit that we raise (our army). Soon the mark in our foreheads will be a common sight to see. A man without a prostration mark will be closely watched in the City, Jerusalem. We are now ready to raise the executioners (our army - Fruit 16 to 30). As we now start to teach, the transformation from the old to the New World will take place, just as it was when the prophet Muhammad, of 1,400 years ago (May the peace and mercy of Allah be with Him and may He ever be one with Allah), when he began to teach a new teaching. The chiefs in Mecca, who thought that they were wise began to fight against the prophet and His followers, because this new teaching would bring an end to their authority over the people. But Muhammad continued to teach until He had enough followers who believed as He believed, then Muhammad and His army of 1,500 executioners, marched into Mecca. Those who had fought the hardest to prevent the transformation, was now at the mercy of Muhammad. This will be the same, or should I say that this history and prophecy is become a reality for us, today. We must fight for the establishment of truth. Mr. Muhammad said February 26, 1960, "Any Muslim who is afraid to fight is no Muslim at all." The prophecy in the Holy Qur'an says that we will be attacked by the old world officials and we are ordered to fight them and kill them as long as they show any sign of opposition to the New World. Read Holy Qur'an 2:190-191 it says quote: "And fight in the way of Allah against those who fight against you but be not aggressive. Surely Allah loves not the aggressors. And kill them wherever you find them, and drive them out from where they drove you out, and persecution is worse than slaughter. And fight not with them at the Sacred Mosque until they fight with you (in it), slay them. Such is the recompense of the disbelievers." End of quote. This prophecy is us today. No one fits this description but us. Just as Jesus is opposed by the chief priest in Jerusalem, the same prophecy in the Holy Qur'an shows the opposition by the same chief priest at the Sacred Mosque (Mosque 25 - God's House).

Our teaching and training of fruit of the New World will produce true believers, warriors, as it states in the Bible's prophecy of Ezekiel 37:10, "So I prophesied as he commanded me, and the breath came into them, and they lived, and stood up upon their feet, an exceeding great army." Our army is dead like the dry bones of Ezekiel, or should I say our army is the dry bones prophesied by the prophet Ezekiel. Again you should read all of the chapter two of Joel, but listen to what verse 11 says: "And the Lord shall utter His voice before His army: for his camp is very great: for he is strong that executeth his word: for the day of the Lord is great and very terrible; and who can abide it?" All of these Divine Prophecies are referring to us today. None of this took place in America before. We are now fulfilling this (the raising of the army of Allah) the executioners, with the mark of the faithful in their foreheads. Read Rev. 9:4-5, "And it was commanded them that they should not hurt the grass of the earth, neither any green thing, neither any tree; but only those men which have not the seal of God in their foreheads. And to them it was given that they should not kill them, but that they should be tormented five months: and their torment was as the torment of a scorpion, when he striketh a man." Read Ezekiel 9:6, "Slay utterly old and young, both maids, and little children, and women: but come not near any man upon whom is the mark; and begin at my sanctuary. Then they began at the ancient men which were before the house." These men before the house, are the chief priests. Also read how we must fight in Jerusalem in Jeremiah 1:19, also read Rev. 19. The Executioners are on the way- on time and in time. Pray, Fast and Teach.

THE END!

11/17/67

Thanks to Allah, for raising from among us, His Last and Greatest Prophet, our Beloved Brother, Master Fard Muhammad, the Saviour.

AL-FARD *THE DAWN*

Thanks to Allah - Thanks, Thanks to Thee, O' Allah, in the person of Master Fard Muhammad who was to come and has come, to restore we who were lost from our own, the kingdom of Islam, and to destroy those who have destroyed us. O' Allah deliver us from our murderers, and we shall serve Thee all the days of our lives, and we will teach our children Thy praise, and to submit to Thee, for Thy unequaled love and mercy for us. And thanks to Thee O' Allah for making manifest our enemy the devil. And bless us, O' Allah, to die the death of Muslims.

As Salaam Alaikum

Bis-mi-illah

A GUIDE TO UNDERSTANDING THE BIBLE AND HOLY QUR'AN
"SUPPLEMENT TO AL-FARD"

Acts 1:2	Foot-note #21 part two .
Acts 1:8	Foot-note #21 part two
Acts 2:32-38	Foot-note #21 part two
Deuteronomy 8:2	Foot-note #9
Deuteronomy 18:18	Foot-note #19
Exodus 4	Foot-note #19
Exodus 6:7	Foot-note #2
Exodus 16:2, 3, 8	Foot-note #19
Exodus 29:45	Foot-note #1
Ezekiel 9:6	Foot-note #25
Ezekiel 37:3, 4	Foot-note #5
Ezekiel 37:10	Foot-note #25
Genesis 13:7	Foot-note #21
Jeremiah 1:19	Foot-note #25
Joel 2:27	Foot-note #5
Joel 3:7	Foot-note #5
Joel 3:17	Foot-note #5

Joel 3:14	Foot-note #15
John 1	Foot-note #3
John 1:11	Foot-note #15
John 1:19-34	Foot-note #2
John 1:29	Foot-note #17
John 1:36	Foot-note #17
John 14:17	Foot-note #14
John 15:26	Foot-note #17
John 16:14	Foot-note #15
John 17:1-4	Foot-note #14
John 17:25-26	Foot-note #14
John 21:15	Foot-note #21 Part 2
Luke 8:18	Foot-note #21
Luke 10:22-24	Foot-note #2
Luke 21:20	Foot-note #18
Luke 24:46-47	Foot-note #21 Part 2
Malachi 4:5	Foot-note #3
Mark 8:27	Foot-note #21
Matthew 11	Foot-note #2
Matthew 11:13-14	Foot-note #2
Matthew 12:31-32	Foot-note #2
Matthew 16:13-21	Foot-note #21 Part 2
Matthew 22:42-45	Foot-note #21
Matthew 24:13	Foot-note #21 Part 2

Matthew 24:14	Foot-note #21 Part 2
Numbers 16:3	Foot-note #21 Part 2
Psalms 82	Foot-note #1
Psalms 110:1	Foot-note #13
Revelations 5	Foot-note #5
Revelations 5:6-9	Foot-note #17
Revelations 9:4-5	Foot-note #25
Revelations 10:5-10	Foot-note #1
Revelations 11	Foot-note #19
Revelations 11:15	Foot-note #1
Revelations 12	Foot-note #18
Revelations 12:4	Foot-note #21 Part 2
Revelations 14	Foot-note #17
Revelations 14:1	Foot-note #17
Revelations 14:1	Foot-note #19
Revelations 15:3	Foot-note #24
Revelations 16:15	Foot-note #21
Revelations 19	Foot-note #25

"THE HOLY QUR'AN"

"The Holy Qur'an referred to is the Translation by Maulana Muhammad Ali 3rd or 4th Edition."

2:190-191	Foot-note #25
2:87	Foot-note #14
3:44	Foot-note #6
5:3	Foot-note #7
7:11-14	Foot-note #4
19:17-21	Foot-note #6
22:7	Foot-note #9
23:54	Foot-note #18
26:10-11	Foot-note #19
28:35	Foot-note #19
48 Section 4	Foot-note #17
112	Foot-note #1

As-Salaam-Alaikum

"A GUIDE TO UNDERSTANDING MESSAGE TO THE BLACKMAN"

The below listed articles can be found in
MESSAGE TO THE BLACKMAN:
the foot-note which contains them in this book are listed below

TITLE	PAGE	FOOT-NOTE
Allah Is Judging Today	28	Foot-note #19
Accept Your Own	46	Foot-note #19
Break-Up of The Old World!	266	Foot-note #15
Battle In The Sky	293	Foot-note #18
Coming Of The Son Of Man	19	Foot-note #11
The Infidels Are Angry	286	Foot-note #18
Fulfillment Of Prophecies Seen	73	Foot-note #4
Islam, Only True Religion Of God	306	Foot-note #9
My Mission Is To Give Life	186	Foot-note #18
Misunderstanding And Misinterpretation	103	Foot-note #23
Making Of The Devil	8	Foot-note #4
Origin Of God As A Spirit And Not A Man	31	Foot-note #9
Original Man, Know Thyself	65	Foot-note #19
Plan To Destroy Our Race	157	Foot-note #19
Prayer For The Messenger	153	Foot-note #19
Prayers To Pray	278	Foot-note #21
Resurrection Of Our People	136	Foot-note #16
Significance Of Prayer	159	Foot-note #17
Confidence Gained Through Prayers	13	Foot-note #13
Coming Of Allah (God)	141	Foot-note #16
Time For Prayer And Its Meaning	177	Foot-note #18
We Must Teach Our Own	48	Foot-note #19

AL-FARD *THE DAWN*

A Guide To Understanding
Message To The Blackman- continued

The below listed articles are enclosed immediately following this page: for easier studying, the foot-note where they are mentioned is also listed below, the date of these articles are included for added convenience.

TITLE	DATE	FOOT-NOTE
The End	Feb. 3. 1962	Foot-note #5
Great Falsehood	Mar. 11/25, 1967	Foot-note #12 & #21
Islam Means Unity!	June 10, 1967	Foot-note #7
In The Hereafter No Medicine No Drugs	Oct. 29, 1965	Foot-note #15
Jesus Prays For His Disciples	July 15, 1966	Foot-note #14
The Truth (Part 6)	Mar. 29, 1962	Foot-note #8
Time And What Must Be Done	June 16, 1967	Foot-note #9
The 144,000	Oct. 20, 1956	Foot-note #17
Jesus A Sign And Example		Foot-note #15
For Wheresoever The Carcass Is, There Shall The Eagles Be Gathered		Foot-note #10
Accept Your Own	Aug. 8, 1964	Foot-note #21
America Hastens Own Doom	Feb. 19, 1966	Foot-note #21

Mr. Muhammad Speaks
February 3, 1962

"THE END"

We are fulfilling that which is written of us in the scriptures (which we must) Read: Matt. 10:23, 5:11, 23, 34. Rev. 12:13.

My followers and I do not belong to the slavemaster anymore. We belong to Allah (God) in whose name we are called; this is universally known. But it is written: "Ye will be persecuted until the help of Allah comes." (Holy Qur'an). That help is very near.

America's jails, I was told, are filled. Some of them are so over crowded that many of the prisoners have to sleep in the hallways. But yet, she (America) rejoices in persecuting the Muslims under false charges, just to discourage our poor blind, deaf and dumb people from accepting the truth (Islam) and returning to their true God, Allah and His true religion, Islam.

"PREY TO GOVERNMENT"

We, the original people, are a prey to the government of America. Who must now be freed and separated from our enemies, the slave masters and their children if we are ever to enjoy peace, freedom, justice and equality.

Twenty million of our people cannot depend upon another nation for existence. We must look to God and self as other nations had to do or continue to beg our enemies (white slave masters) for jobs to exist among them, instead of asking and demanding a chance to go for self and create our own jobs.

This is a disgrace to the leadership of twenty million people who do not want the responsibility of caring for self. Well the time is very near when you'll have to do for self.

"SOMETHING OF PAST"

America and the entire white race's ruling power over the brown, red, yellow and Black nations of Africa and Asia will soon be something of the past. No longer will these nations bow to the Western Powers. America's doom is sealed and is inevitable, according to the word of Allah (God) to me.

Allah desires to make Himself known to the world, that He alone is God and has appeared among us in the person of Master W. Fard Muhammad.

Both the Bible and Holy Qur'an teach of the presence of God in person at the end of the world of Satan, the devil's rule. We would be foolish to disbelieve that such character is not present and is not directing the course of the nation's today.

"ALLAH AGAINST WHITES"

The American white race is the number one people whom Allah's anger is directed against as Jehovah's anger was against Egypt in the time of Moses. Jehovah's weapons of war used against Pharaoh and his people were the forces of nature: flies, frogs, lice, diseases, rains, hailstones, fire, water and finally the drowning of Pharaoh and his armies in the Red Sea.

The same forces of nature are prepared to be used against America. Terrifying storms (which now harass America); the loss of friendship of the nations, a specially prepared enemy people under the name "Gog" and "Magog", whose skill and power will cover the earth for a while: there will be no friends for America; snow, ice and earthquakes, even droughts and dust storms, the natural powers of water, wind, terrific cold out of the north, fire from the sun, agitation of the high seas by the magnetism of the Moon and Sun (which will aid in the destruction of America's sea power).

"SINS ARE GREATEST'

This is referred to in the prophecy of Jesus, read Luke 21:25, also Isaiah 27:1, Rev. 8:7-9. America's sins are the greatest. Her sins are even worse than all the nations of the earth combined. She sees and knows her doom is near.

So, she seeks to trick her slaves (so-called Negroes) to share this doom with her. But she knows that her once slaves have a chance of escaping, so she hypocritically offers them social equality under the "integration" which she knows the blind, deaf and dumb will fall, while it is an open trap of death for both sides.

My people do not realize this nor will they believe this until they are hurt or it is too late.

This is the work of Allah, not you and I. Read your Bible and Holy Qur'an. America has always hated and mistreated her slaves (so-called Negroes). Today, she backs up the police departments throughout the country to beat and kill poor blackmen and women.

We have always been submissive to these cruel, merciless enemies like lambs to a pack of hungry wolves. Stop tricking your slaves, white America, separate them into a good place on some of this soil that you robbed our people of with superior weapons and supply them with that which is necessary to get started for self.

Then, maybe your doom will be delayed awhile, otherwise Allah will do it and will not leave a place for you anywhere on the planet.

It is not the evils done to others by the white race of America, Allah wishes to make America an example of His judgment, that both Europe and Asia may know that He alone is God and has redeemed the helpless Black slaves from their merciless enemies.

I have warned you, take it or leave it.

Peace . . . Peace . . .

Mr. Muhammad Speaks
March 11, 1967

"THE GREAT FALSEHOOD"

Since the birth and death of Jesus, there has been more false stories told about him than any other prophet.

The false worship of the birthday of Jesus is one of them. No one knows exactly when he was born, except Mary and Joseph, his mother and father. God, in the person of Master Fard Muhammad, to Whom praise is due forever told me that it most certainly did not take place on the 25th day of December. They kept it a secret because of Herod's desire to kill him at birth. The actual day of the week has never been made known. However, they know that he was born either the first or the second week of September.

The Christian theologians will agree with me that they do not know the exact day of his birth. They also agree that it could not have taken place in the month of December. This is verified according to the history and scriptures pertaining to his birth.

Some Christians begin preparing two and three months in advance for this false worship of Allah's (God's) most righteous and perfect prophet of the past. They store up wine to drink in the worship of the prophet, Jesus, of whom they preach and represent as being God and the equal of his sender, Allah (God).

Farmers in the southern, eastern and western sections of the country pen up filthy swine, the divinely prohibited flesh, in order to fatten them for eating purposes pertaining to the worship of the great prophet, Jesus, who condemned the eating of the swine.

2000 years before the birth of Jesus, Allah through Moses, divinely prohibited Israel from eating the filthy swine. It is the most prized dish on the menu of the Christian world, which claims to be like Jesus and his true representatives.

If Jesus were able to return on the 25th day of December and see how his name and his teachings are being disgraced by a race of infidels he would say, "I thought Allah would have destroyed you for your evil and murder of me and my disciples, 2,000 years ago."

Today it is made manifest, the Christians are greater teachers of falsehood and worshippers of images than any other religious worshippers in the world. They preach against and condemn false worshippers. Yet, they do the same in a greater and more modern way of worship than did those of ancient times.

They make statues of Jesus and his twelve disciples, although, they have never had a true picture or true piece of sculpture of them, as there was none available in that day and time. Yet, they give us a false picture and a false piece of sculpture and they bow down and worship these pictures and statues, contrary to the commandment of God, they also make false pictures and false statues of Mary, the mother, of the Holy Prophet Jesus.

Christianity teaches the false conception of Jesus - that he was born without the agency of a man. They honor a false death of Jesus - that nails were driven through his hands and feet while he was still alive, that a wreath of thorns was placed on his head in mockery of a crown and that he died, hanging on a cross and that he was speared through the heart by one of Herod's soldiers. All of this is false. Allah said he was killed by a deputy sheriff.

They teach that after his most torturous murder, he was taken down, put into a grave and that three days later angels came and rolled away the stone which covered the grave - that he left his disciples 40 days after this rising from a literal death and grave and was seen by his disciples ascending up into open space with the same body and wounds from the nails and holes through his heart which was made by the spear of the Roman soldier.

Mr. Muhammad Speaks
March 18, 1967

"THE GREAT FALSEHOOD"

Ignorant people all over the world, who are misinformed and who have misinterpreted the scriptures, take these great falsehoods to be actual truth. If it is turned around into something realistic and the fantasy taken away, perhaps some truth could be found somewhere.

Allah (God) who came in the person of Master Fard Muhammad, to whom praise is due forever, taught me the truth. Jesus, with his consent, was stabbed to death so that his name and his true teachings would live until the coming of the Great Mahdi, God in Person, who would come to destroy those who have destroyed and murdered the prophets and the righteous. This is now being fulfilled.

The Great Falsehood is that the people are looking for him to return as the same man he was 2,000 years ago. The general understanding of the Christian teachings causes converts to worship a God and Jesus that does not exist - false ones who cannot be truthfully proven. They direct the minds of the people into space and to un-seen and un-heard spirits. They teach that Jesus is living somewhere in space sitting on the right hand of God, the father, until the unleashing of the wrath and judgment of God upon the devil and followers.

The Great Mahdi, this is the fulfillment of the prophecy of the coming of the Son of Man, the Great Messiah. This is the Jesus of the second coming a man, same ideas, that Jesus had concerning the infidels - that they Should be destroyed and removed from the face of the earth - for there is no good in them. Jesus declared, "No, not one is good." How can one of them be good? The very nature in which they were made was not good.

See the evil way in which they celebrate the 25th day of December - ugly, drunk, vomiting, cursing, swearing, gambling, fighting, shooting and cutting each other to death. They pray and preach of the birth of the Holy Jesus while they are under the influence of wine, whiskey and beer and their tables will be laden with fresh killed hog meat cooked in various ways. They will eat the divinely prohibited flesh and drink intoxicating drinks - all of this is done in the worship of God, and His righteous prophet, Jesus.

Today, we see the whole Christian church gambling and taking part in games of chance. It is impossible to find a holy assembly, of the people called Christians or sincere followers of Jesus. In their drunken gathering, you will find deadly weapons such as knives and pistols on their persons.

And all types of gambling devices, playing cards and drugs are found on their persons. Then they dismiss from the church and go to filthy dancing parties and continue their worship of the holy prophet. Such wickedness and mockery of Allah's (God's) divine prophet, Jesus, justifies God's destruction of the Christian world.

Just think of a people enslaved for three (3) centuries without any knowledge of any realization - without a knowledge of reading and writing, without any education at all and then an enemy gives them a book with all of this in it, and gives it to the slave and to the world, as though it was the truth, as written. God, taught me that the present Bible is not in accordance with the original scripture and how they should be understood. The scholars and theologians give the English translations of the Bible between 465 - 470 years ago. If you will spend a little of your time on the research of Christianity and its people, you will find that from the very beginning of the organization of this religion, it was based on falsehood.

Mr. Muhammad Speaks
March 25, 1967

"THE GREAT FALSEHOOD"

The better knowledge of the scriptures was in Hebrew and Greek. It was put into symbols which made it hard for the unlearned, and uneducated and undivine to understand - until God gave to them one from Himself, who had been taught by him, the understanding of the book. This is the only way that the truth could be given and taught from a book in which the truth had been tampered with by the enemy of truth.

The so-called Negro is blessed today with the truth from the mouth of God. But, the false teaching and misunderstanding of the Bible by the preacher blinds the so-called Negro to the extent that he thinks his spiritual blindness is the true light of God.

****

If Jesus were able to return on the 25th day of December and see how his name and teachings are being disgraced by a race of infidels, he would say, "I thought Allah would have destroyed you for your evil and murder of me and my disciples, 2,000 years ago."

****

The children are reared up under spiritually blind parents, who continue the false teaching by teaching them that on the 24th day of December a Santa Claus will visit them bearing presents while they are asleep. They make great pictures, from statues and dress men in red uniforms with long white beards. This is to call attention again to Jesus and disciples, through this color. They point everything towards heaven, God, His Prophet and angels.

Christianity teaches the false conception of Jesus - that he was born without the agency of a man.

The Great Falsehood is that the people are looking for him to return as the same man that he was 2,000 years ago. The general understanding of the Christian teachings causes converts to worship a God and Jesus that does not exist - false one who cannot be truthfully proven.

****

They tell the children "Go to sleep, Santa Claus is coming." They represent him in pictures as coming to children on a sled drawn by several deers. They tell them that he comes down the chimney with a great bag of toys. The parents place toys besides their beds and in their stockings. The children are born and raised in falsehood from the ancient worship of falsehood, that, "when you die, you will go to heaven somewhere in space." This is the final falsehood.

****

The so-called Negro is blessed today with the truth from the mouth of God.

The truth is, the parents are the Santa Claus, and the children are taught to give credit to a false giver. Therefore, the parents are robbing themselves of the true credit, that is due to them from their children, in the same way that Allah (God) is being robbed of the true worship.

So, if you will spend a little of your time on the research of Christianity and its people, you will find that from the very beginning of the organization of this religion, it was based on falsehood.

In Rome where the father of the church sits, there is the great

Christian worship of the stars and cattle. The cow is worshipped in both the Christian and Hindu religions.

Think of what you are doing on the 24th and 25th day of December, under a good name, Jesus, the last Prophet sent to the Jews or the Caucasian world in general - THE GREAT FALSEHOOD.

Peace... Peace...

Mr. Muhammad Speaks
June 10, 1967

"ISLAM MEANS UNITY"

The true religion of Islam is being offered for the first time to us, the lost-found members of our nation, by God Himself.

The teachings of God's only true religion (Islam) are for the purpose of qualifying to return to the Nation of Islam to which we belong by nature, but from which we were deceived and brought out of by the devils.

Islam is not a religion that has dominated the white race (devils) because they were not created by nature to be a righteous people.

Islam is a religion for the righteous. The devils, were not created by nature to accept righteousness. They cannot be righteous. Jesus made this clear when he was trying to reform the white race (devils) 2000 years ago. (John 8:37 and 47).

The white race (devils) have deceived the darker people of the earth in proposing that they came from the God of Righteousness and are equal with the righteous, by having been created by the God of Righteousness. This they say, but if you and I believe they are from the God of Righteousness, we are making the God of Righteousness a God of evil who would create an evil god to become His enemy as the best way of guiding His people and keeping them on the right path.

Islam is being offered to us to show us who the enemy is and who the friend is.

He comes in Person, to teach us the right way and to point out to us the great arch-deceiver (white devils). This is the most hated truth that they are opposing in the last days (resurrection of the mentally dead).

They are bringing themselves into the judgment of God, Himself, by trying, to take vengeance in the last days on the Apostle of Truth and His followers.

****

Messengers are never sent. They are always raised in the midst of those whom Allah warns so they cannot claim that they did not understand the language of the Messenger or say that he was a foreigner or stranger. The Messenger is one from them.

****

God has given Islam to us in order to guide us into His infinite Wisdom. It is the wisdom, the divine wisdom of God, that puts us on the path to ascend to the heights that He has vouched for us as being safe for us.

This is the great wisdom that God promised us through His prophets - the wisdom that would make us the head and no longer the tail.

It is prophesied in the Bible. (Isaiah 60:1-2) "Arise and shine, for the light has come." This is the first time that the light of truth, the knowledge of self, and the knowledge of the enemy of self and God has been made manifest. This is also the first manifestation of the cause of the spiritual darkness that we have lived in for the past six thousand years.

The light of truth has come to us in the Person of Master Fard Muhammad.

****

Islam is being offered to us to show us who the enemy is and who the friend is.

ALI MAHDI MUHAMMAD

****

God in person, to whom praises are due forever. He offers to take off the yoke of bondage of Satan, the devil, and the chains of slavery and give to us the key that will always be available to us - a key that can keep us out of the prison cells of Satan, the devil.

Peace... Peace...

Mr. Muhammad Speaks
October 29, 1965

"IN THE HEREAFTER: NO MEDICINE: NO DRUGS"

The teachings of what the people who are trying to qualify for the Hereafter will be and do, begins with the coming of Allah (God) according to many prophecies of the Bible and hints found in the Holy Qur'an readings and studies.

Since this world (white race) was not to follow Divine Laws or Rules for the good of man (The Black Man), they were to teach and operate a civilization that never was tried and experienced by the Original Nation of the earth (the Black Man). In the beginning of the white race's rule over the Black Nation, the Black Nation was forced to give their wisdom and knowledge of how the Black Man operated and ruled civilization for themselves on the basis of justice, righteousness, and prolongation of life skills; science in buildings and constructing civilization. According to our history of the Gods and the worlds that they build, everyone is left to use his own idea of what type of world he will build without the knowledge of any previous builders. Note the beginning awakening of the Blackman is very swift. This is due to the fact that he once was a great original ruler.

His scientists can set themselves in order under the guidance of that Mighty One, whom the world has been looking for to come and head the change over to the construction of a New World with new laws and rules to govern the New World - making the progress fast but with sure success. Therefore, we cannot look forward to furthering the way of life of this people who follow the rules and laws of the god of this world to build what you have experienced of this world and are still experiencing. No pattern of a former world is allowed by a new God, who has ideas and Wisdom which are latent in Him, and which, if given a chance, can build something different.

These civilizations and worlds headed by the Gods of the past, reigned or ruled the people according to the circumference of our earth, which is approximately 25,000 miles. Therefore, they build history to last for 25,000 years. But, this new world, which is prophesied of will put an end to temporary kingdoms; as the Holy Qur'an and Bible refers to the Mahdi or the Messiah (God in Person) AS BEING WISER THAN THEM ALL. He will build a civilization and government with infinite wisdom that will live forever.

This is the world that is emerging from the old world. This is what we are being qualified for. There will be no poison medicine or drugs used in that world to decay the life of the people.

Natural laws will be obeyed, as Islam is the natural religion of the Original Blackman - it being the natural religion of the natural man. The nature of the man and the religion of the man are the same. For this is the very life of the man or creature who was created by the law of which he was created. It is natural for the man to obey the law of in which he was created. Therefore, going back to the law of nature means there will be no place for medicine or drugs.

As I have said time and again, these are the first steps being taken in what we should eat; how we should eat and when we should eat - at the same time creating in the body new material of thinking to feed the brain with proper mental food which serves as security against physical attacks of foreign and strange matter that would always be present in combat with and against the natural laws of nature. Everything happens on time and in time.

Peace... Peace...

Mr. Muhammad Speaks
July 15, 1966

"JESUS PRAYS FOR HIS DISCIPLES"

In John 17:1 - Jesus said, "The hour is come." What hour does Jesus refer to? (It could not have referred to the judgment of his enemies). Does it refer to Jesus's death (more likely his death) or to the doom of his enemies? Or does it refer to victory, (if a victory, where was it won)? (An accomplishment of his mission?) (His mission to convert the Jews was not accomplished).

"Glorify Thy Son, that Thy Son also may glorify Thee." Here the demand for glorification is on condition that God glorify the Son first and the Son will glorify the God or the Father. Here also it is made clear that without glorification of the Son there could be none for the Father.

The language used in the first verse of John 17 can easily be taken as one speaking of someone else other than himself. If referring to self the words: "Glorify Me Thy Son."

The second is contrary to the verses - 8,9,12 for he says in the second verse "As Thou has given him (not me) power over all flesh, (whose flesh? - not the Jews) that he (not self) should give eternal life to as many as Thou hast given him." (Not the words to me).

In John 17:24 these words "Thou hast given Me." (Here it is made clear one is speaking of self (me). But how did the mix-up of English come about?

I only want to show that Jesus was only a prophet.

Peace... Peace...

Mr. Muhammad Speaks
March 29, 1962

"THE TRUTH" PART 6

"O Apostle, deliver what has been revealed to you from your Lord; and if you do it not, then you have not delivered His message, and Allah will protect you from the people." (Holy Qur'an 5:67.)

When Allah God decides to reveal His Truth and bring an end to falsehood, that truth must be delivered regardless of the cost! The Messenger of truth should not fear to deliver it if that truth is from Allah, He will be the protector of it as well as the protector of the Messenger who delivers it (truth). A true Messenger of Allah never fears to deliver the message of Allah, nor does he ever fail to deliver it - even though most of them (Messengers) and their followers suffered severe persecution, even death, yet the message of Allah was delivered.

The awakening of the Arabs nearly fourteen hundred years ago to the ancient truth (Islam) (not a new truth). Muhammad and his work is typical of what will be done today. He was opposed by the Arabs for awhile. Although the Arab Nation and their country was the birth place of the Great Prophets and the Scriptures, and from there prophets are sent throughout the world from the time of Adam until today. The Arab history cannot be compared with the history of the so-called Negroes who have never had a Divine Prophet nor a Scripture!

According to the past histories of the major prophets, one comes every 2,000 years until the end of the world of sin. Moses came exactly 2,000 years until the end of the world of sin. Moses came exactly 2,000 years after Yakub (the God and maker of the evil

Caucasian race). Jesus came 2,000 years after Moses and the last prophet came 2,000 years after Jesus, fulfilling much of the histories of the prophets before him; especially Moses, David, Jesus and Muhammad. The man Allah (God) raised up from among the American so-called Negroes in the west will unite his people to Islam with the guidance of Allah, with a Book of scriptures for his people prepared and written by the finger of Allah (God).

His teachings will be called a New Islam and will be opposed by many who would not like a change from the old to a higher knowledge of the Divine. The present Holy Qur'an Sharrieff leads us right up to the door of the final book for our future though not admitting us in: yet we are able to get a glance at some things.

The devil (white race) watches the believers, and when he finds one showing any sign of weakness, he helps him become more weaker in the faith. Islam is the greatest unifying force on the Planet Earth. Islam is a religion that is backed by its Author, Allah, to Whom be Praise Forever. Islam could save the world from its destructive fall, but the world has practiced evil so long that she would rather go to her doom than to turn and do righteousness. Look at the silly things the world is doing, "working like mad" to destroy each other! For what?

Is not there enough earth for every one of us? Yes, there is enough if we would be satisfied with our share, and not seek to rob the other man of his share. Billions of dollars are being spent for the purpose of destroying humanity from the face of the earth: which is nothing but a waste of money that could be spent for the happiness of the Nations and not for their death. The wicked will be the losers!

Peace... Peace...

Mr. Muhammad Speaks
June 16, 1967

"THE TIME AND WHAT MUST BE DONE"

What must be done about the 22 million or more so-called Negroes, the Lost and Now Found People of our kind, the aboriginal race in this time in North America? What must be done with the world that we have known, and of the separation of the nation's now taking place which so much concerns us, Black People?

The day of which I have been warning you for over 36 years is here. Still you wait. You wish to find falsehood in what I teach. Why can't you open your eyes and see the great works and great reforms taking place in many of my followers, whom Almighty Allah, God, has enabled me to teach? It must be clear to you that I am not alone, and that there is a God with me. I want you to remember that I have always taught that you should return to your own God, and people. You have before you today radio and television evidence clearly showing and warning you that what I, Elijah Muhammad, has taught you is most certainly the truth.

We must be separated. We must be reformed according to the truth. You must realize this. These are now the days which are prophesied in both the Bible and Holy Qur'an. But have you paid any attention to these prophecies? No. I call to your attention one great prophecy in your Bible, which is now coming to pass. Let us read it, St. Luke 21:20. "And when you shall see Jerusalem compassed with armies, then know that the desolation thereof is nigh." The 21st verse of the same chapter! "Then let them that are in Judea flee to the mountains; and let them which are in the midst of it depart out; and let not them that are in the countries enter there into." The 22nd verse of the same chapter: "For these be the days of vengeance, that all things which are written may be fulfilled."

We see this now coming to pass. We see Jerusalem compassed with armies. We see the nations of the earth setting themselves for the slaughter of one another. We see the fulfilling of Daniels' prophecy. Wherein he prophesied that desolation after the war "desolation is determined." We see this now on the way. We see that a great separation has now begun, as also prophesied.

The citizens of America are being removed by the East, to go to their homes, never to return to the East again. This is the judgment of the world. I have taught this to you day and night for the past 36 years. But you are too proud of yourselves. You want a home with your slavemasters. You seem to think that it is human enough if you can live in their neighborhoods.

However great and rich, this is a falling nation. You will be falling with it. If God puts forth His hand against you, the matter is settled. Jerusalem is no longer a Holy City. The time is now that everyone who does not belong in that area must fly. We know how the Jews got into Jerusalem a few years ago. In the time of Moses, the Jews were given Israel on condition that they obey all the laws and rules that Allah gave them. They fell away. They could not live up to the law of Moses. Moses gave the law to them, but none of them kept it.

This is the day that shall prove these words of prophecy. Study the prophecies of both the Bible and the Holy Qur'an and you will learn that you are living in the days of the judgment of this world.

If Israel should conquer the Arabs that they could govern them for a while, this will not mean that she will be the ruler or even the part ruler of the East. She cannot make liars out of God and His Prophets.

This has been put in black and white in their Bible. It is in the Holy Qur'an that there must be a day of reckoning with these people in the East.

And that day is now, according to the Bible. It is very plain in the 21st chapter verses 20:21 and 22 of St. Luke. It could not be better fulfilled. Who is it that flees to the mountains out of Judea, and to what mountains? Should we take the word mountain literally? Are the Jews or the Arabs to fly out of Judea into the mountains? What are the mountains?

The mountains here do not mean the mountains in Judea. These mountains are the great powers of those that are already there now to assist.

Peace... Peace...

Mr. Muhammad Speaks
October 20, 1956

"THE HUNDRED FORTY-FOUR THOUSAND"
"THE LAMB - NEGROES NAMES"

This number is mentioned in the Bible (Rev. 14:1) as being the number of the first believers in Allah (God) and His Messenger. The Messenger is called the Lamb due to certain characteristics of His (Messenger) being similar to that of a sheep, and the tender love of Allah for him like that of a good shepherd toward his sheep - though the love of Allah (God) for the so-called Negroes is not equaled by anyone. Describing us as sheep is about the best way of putting it, for sheep are dumb, ignorant and humble, not aggressive. They will not fight even if attacked by the wolf. So are the so-called Negroes and Allah has to do the fighting for them.

Let us understand what we are reading. It is prophecy in symbolic revelation of the Bible that was seen in a vision by Yakub, the father of the white race, which he saw on the Isle of Patmos or Pelan, 6,000 years ago. He was warning his people of that which would come to them at the end of their time.

The number (144,000) in mathematics means a square which is a perfect answer for the work of Allah (God) with a number of people. They are the first (Negro) from among the wicked to Allah (God) and His Messenger, referred to as the first ripe fruit (the first of the righteous) unto God and the Lamb, in verse 4 of the same chapter. They are righteous enough (ripe) to be picked out of the wicked race to be used for the purpose of squaring the nations of the earth to righteousness. After the righteous Black Nation has labored under the rule of the wicked devils for 6,000 years, the return of a righteous ruler under the God of righteousness, the people must be re-organized to live under such a government. The All-Wise God,

Allah to whom praise is due, who came in the Person of Master Fard Muhammad, is seeking us the lost and last members of the chosen nation, is building a New World of Righteousness out of the old. Therefore, He lays the base of His Kingdom with a square number of mathematics, Truth. His New World of Islam (Kingdom of Peace) can be proven mathematically step by step, which we all know mathematics is truth.

They had the names of their Father, not the beasts' names (slavemaster) which was of no value, his names and works are to be destroyed from the earth. The beasts' name was not a name of God nor His attributes, but this the so-called Negroes don't know, but I am telling you now, all Muslim names have a beautiful meaning and 99 of them are Divine Attributes. Remember my people Jones, Johnson, Smith, Hog, Bird, Fish, Bear, Woods and such names as Roundtree will not be accepted, by your God and mine Allah.

To make that square (144,000), to be truthful with you, God said that He will not accept any white people in His Kingdom. The mark according to the Holy Qur'an that will be in their foreheads will be from prostrating, the Muslims prostrate in their prayers on rough floors or rugs, which produces a mark on their forehead. "Some of my followers have such a sign now produced by the five-prayers-a-day obligation."

The righteous is always marked by his righteousness, as the wicked is marked by his or her acts. "They are actually marked by nature and are recognized by both parties."

The 144,000 were not afraid of the beast, as God is on their side and they put their trust in Him alone. The Lamb (Messenger) only weapon was the truth (the sword that proceeded out of his mouth) and it stands true that truth alone is sufficient to destroy falsehood, as light destroys darkness. The ninth verse of the same chapter (Rev.

14) warns us against worshipping the beast, his image or to receive his mark on our head or in our hand, "and the same shall drink the wrath of God, which is poured out without mixture: and he shall be tormented with fire and brimstone in the presence of the holy angels and the Lamb (Apostle)". The so-called Negroes have great love for their slavemaster, their churches, religion, color and works. This love must be lost or cast away to become one of the 144,000. You who believe, literally in the physical resurrection of the dead must remember that the book teaches here that the first righteous to be saved (the 144,000) is redeemed from among men (Rev. 14:4) not out of the grave. It is a sin that you are so blinded that you cannot see, nor will you accept "plain truth". Surely there is a resurrection of the dead.

It is one of the principles of Islam, but not the physical dead in the graveyards. It is the mentally dead; the ignorant whom the devils falsehood has killed, to the knowledge of truth, the Divine Truth which must be preached to them to awaken them into the knowledge of him again.

You and I know that it can't refer to a physically dead person, because that one won't and cannot rise again. What is left to rise from a body that has gone back to the earth, or up into smoke, or eaten by some wild beast or fish of the sea? People who died before the flood: and after, even Adam, they have nothing to rise from. Remember the Old Testament (Torah) doesn't teach of a resurrection of the dead, according to Job (Chapter 7:9) "He that goeth down into the grave shall come up no more." He must be right as we haven't seen one come up from the grave that was really dead. Surely, if it had meant a physical death God would have taught it to Adam, Noah, Abraham, Moses and all the ancient prophets would have had a knowledge of it, even Job, not so.

You have two Jesus histories as I have said time and again; and even an Apostle's history of the last days, all under the name of

Jesus, 2,000 years ago.

Of course, there are many student ministers in the theological seminary colleges, who probably know, or are learning, that most of what the Bible gives us of Jesus history has got to be a future man and not one answering any such description of 2,000 year ago.

Peace... Peace...

Mr. Muhammad Speaks

"JESUS A SIGN AND EXAMPLE"

I am so happy that Allah (God) has revealed to me the truth, believe it or not. Oh you die-hard Christians, you are stubborn and proud against Allah (God) and His word. My people are deaf, dumb and blind; and greatly poisoned by the enemy (devil). Use common sense my people and judge between the truth, which I am writing, and the false that was taught to you by the devils.

Jesus came as a sign of that which was to come. His birth, ministry, persecution and death were signs of the persecution and death, as I have written, the future of you (the so-called Negroes) his people; and the persecution and rejection of the Great Mahdi (God) (in person) who has appeared among us in these last days of this race of devils, and has suffered the same.

Jesus was an example of righteousness, a doer of the law of the Jews, which was given to them by Musa (Moses). The world looking for that Jesus to return is not only ignorant but foolish. No one but a fool would believe that Jesus, who was here 2,000 years ago, is sitting in heaven waiting for his time to return and execute judgment. Tell the world the truth and stop fooling yourself if you know it; if you don't know it, step aside and stop trying to hinder us who are telling the truth.

The Bible makes it a little too hard for the average reader to believe in Jesus as a prophet, or a man born by the agency of man, like you and I; though never did God intend otherwise. The Holy Qur'an makes Jesus only a prophet of Allah (God); and, that was all he was. It does not mention his father by name, though on many occasions prophets and their great works of the past are mentioned without their father's names. There are many Muslims who think that his birth was without the agency of man. Most commentators on the life and death of Jesus disagree with the saying that "Jesus died on the cross" or even was murdered (killed). They think that he traveled into India and died in Kashmir, but this is wrong. He did not go there, nor is that his tomb in Kashmir, it is only an old belief among those who did not know who the Nabi (Prophet) was, who came to Kashmir and died and was buried there, who old settlers claimed came from the west. No real proof is shown that it was Jesus's body. The scholars on the Holy Qur'an go to the extreme with the word "spirit", as the Christians do, especially in the case of Allah. My work is to bring you face to face with God, and do away with spooky beliefs. The revealing of the spiritual word of Allah (God) to Mary or anyone, does not mean for you and me to believe that Jesus was born without the agency of man. The spirit or word of Allah (God) came to Moses's mother, to inform her about the future of her son (that he was a prophet) Exodus 2:2. Both the Bible and Holy Qur'an seem to be very careful not to accuse Mary of fornication. Why? If she and her son were to be a sign for the Nation, she could not be charged with fornication. (2nd) If the act was to serve as a lesson to us, that we should never allow two people who are in love with each other to be alone together, in a place where there is no others for nature has no self-control.

That was the case of Mary and Joseph. They were childhood sweethearts, and wanted to be married when of age; but Mary's father objected to it. To this day, the Muslims keep their boys and girls, men and women, from mixing freely together. Even the boy and girl courtships and marriages are controlled by their parents. There is no fornication, and very little or no divorce cases in the dominant Muslim world. That is why Islam is hated by white Christian devils, because they are not allowed to mix with Muslim women: with their filthy, indecent hearts, and winking blue eyes.

"We breathed into her our inspiration, and made her and her son a sign for the nations." Holy Qur'an 21:91

Regardless of careful language of their scripture, used on Mary, having a baby out of wedlock, we can see through it all: after knowledge from Allah (God) in the person of Master Fard Muhammad (to whom be praise forever). In another chapter it mentions the spirit sent to Mary in the form of a man. "So she screened herself from them. Then we sent to her, Our spirit and it appeared to her as a well-made man." Holy Qur'an 19:17.

Peace... Peace...

Mr. Muhammad Speaks

"FOR WHERESOEVER THE CARCASS IS, THERE SHALL THE EAGLES BE GATHERED MATT. 24:28"

The poor so-called Negroes are the mentally dead carcass of the Nation. The robbers of them, even their kind, come from every direction to eat (rob) them. Their enemies, (the white slavemasters) bleached them as a dried bone for 400 years. Yet their own kind seek to grind the bones which are left. They are blind, deaf and dumb, and every civilized person who finds them soon discovers that they are prey; and go after them like eagle birds to finish them off. It is a shame and a sin on the robbers of my people. I find robbers of them from black, brown, yellow, red and white races. They come from all walks of life, from the gamblers, dope peddlers, to the religious leaders of all faiths and their members; even to the weak Muslim of America and Asia, not to mention the Christian leaders who have eaten the flesh and left the bones for the foreigners.

The presence of Allah (God), who wants to put flesh again on their bleached bones and life in me and those who follow me, has caused many eagles to come flying; seeking to get-hold on what is left of them. They would like to charge me WITH GRINDING THE BONES OF MY PEOPLE, but they cannot, even after honeycombing my followers with dirty paid stool pigeons, many of them with me now recognize and only wait the hour to rid ourselves of them. The eagles of prey envy the shepherd of God among them because the shepherd will fight for the safety of his sheep, and he has Allah (God) on his side. He is appointed by Allah (God) and Allah has given him the sheep to feed with the bread of truth, and will not give them to anyone else. Some of the eagles (robbers) even seek the help of religious scholars here and there to say that they are the ones who shall or should be this people to us from God. But this is not so. You cannot send or authorize anyone to cover this job of giving life to my people regardless to whom you are, or where you came from. Allah is the sender of His Messenger.

Many of the eagles (robbers) have nothing to offer but arguments against the shepherd, telling the sheep that he (the shepherd) is not the Messenger of Allah and that he is not an Apostle. They say, he is not teaching Islam, he is teaching hate." He cannot speak or read the Arabic language. They so foolishly do not know that the Holy Qur'an and Bible have all their evil sayings and doings recorded in them. "And those who disbelieve say: you are not the Messenger. Say: Allah is sufficient for a witness between you and me and whosoever has knowledge of the book." Holy Qur'an 13:43. Muhammad could not read or write, but was granted the revelation which made up the Book called the Holy Qur'an. He was given the knowledge by Allah, who gave it to him. Take a look at Allah's servant in the Bible, it says: "Who is blind as he that is perfect, and as blind as the Lord's servant? Seeing many things, but those observest not; opening the ears, but he hearest not. The Lord is well pleased for his righteous sake; he will magnify the law, and make it honorable."

No prophet of the past brought forth judgment unto truth. Judgment for truth sake, comes at the end of the world. Jesus and Muhammad both failed to convert the Jews and Christians, but the Last Messenger - will not make an attempt to convert them. His teachings are to close the door against the enemies of Allah (God) and His prophet.

Judgment follows his message for God is left to act after him. He is the end of the prophets because there is nothing left for a prophet to do after God has manifested Himself to the world. Along with the last Messenger.

ALI MAHDI MUHAMMAD

Peace... Peace...

Mr. Muhammad Speaks
August 8, 1964

"ACCEPT YOUR OWN"

In the last issue of this paper, this subject, Accept Your Own, brought us into the knowledge that we have not had our own, and explains that even today with all of our white civilized schooling, we have not been taught of our own, they will never teach us of our own.

Since the coming of Allah, their reason for not teaching us of our own is made crystal clear. The knowledge that Allah has given us gives the knowledge of our own, being the first people of the earth, we are destined to be the last, we are the creators and makers. This limited civilization of the white man and his rule is now terminating to never be brought into existence again. This rule makes it absolutely against the will of the white man to honor and respect you and me and our Nation as being the first people and the makers of the universe.

Why so much teaching and warning given to the American so-called Negroes and so little or no teaching of the kind being given to the African and Asian Black Nation? It is due to the fact that we are living in the midst of a people whom Allah (God) will destroy in the very near future. We are on the brink of fire and must be removed to a zone of safety. The ignoring of such warning and of the time of the judgment of this world (the Caucasian world with their great universal power that they have exercised over the Black Nation) makes it very hard for the average Black person to conceive the idea of such a strong race of people being removed. This is a very small thing in the eyes and power of Allah, to remove and destroy people who have brought his anger against them for their neglect of worship and respect of Him as the Supreme Being, and they do not even respect His Representatives, but persecute and kill them.

This people have been the worst people to us (the Black Nation) since they have been on the face of the earth. They were created and made for just that purpose of destroying our peace as well as our lives. They have destroyed 600,000,000 of the Black Nation since they have been on our planet. This averages 100,000,000 every thousand years of their rule. They have affected 9/10 of the total population of the Black man under their rule, including the brown, red, and yellow races. They have deceived as the Bible (Revelations of John) says - the whole world, and now they are being made manifest as the deceivers and adversaries of Allah and His true religion of entire submission to His will (Islam).

The Black people of America who have been swallowed up symbolically by the white slavemaster and his children, must now be brought out of this race of people and be taught the knowledge of their own. Allah is holding the affair in person under the name of Master Fard Muhammad. He has chosen us today to be His people and means to take us and build and establish forever, a people of righteousness and a people with unlimited knowledge of the Divine Supreme Being. The very least one of these will become greater than the greatest of this world.

The Orthodox Muslims will have to bow to the choice of Allah. Allah will bring about a New Islam. As for the principles of belief, they will remain the same. There will be no more signs to be watched for the coming of God and the setting up a New World of Islam. We are seeing the change now and entering into it, the devils oppose this change and the Orthodox join them in opposing us because of their desire to carry on the old ways of Islam.

Allah will place those of His choice in authority in the making of the New World and others must obey whoever He puts in authority or find themselves fighting against the power of whom they hold to be on their side and in their favor. We must have a New World, we accept for a New Nation completely. As Yakub brought about a people (the present white race) who are a completely new people made out of the Original of us, another new people must be made to be the ruling voice of tomorrow out of this old world that is now living her last days.

They will be a completely new people. The Holy Qur'an and Bible refer to them as being brought about by the power and will of God in person in the resurrection of the mentally dead, lost-found Original People in America. We may not seem to please you or be pleasing to Allah, but it is written in the Bible that He has chosen us, and repeatedly, He says in the Holy Qur'an and Bible that He will give to whom He pleases and chastise whom He pleases.

This is to warn us that we have no choice in the matter. Whatever Allah desires, He will bring it into being, whether we like it or not. I hope to see you in Los Angeles on Sunday, August, 1964, at the Olympia Auditorium where the finishing touch to this article will be given.

Peace... Peace...

Mr. Muhammad Speaks
February 19, 1966

"AMERICA HASTENS OWN DOOM"

The ultimate aim of this world should be known to everyone; especially the righteous. We classify the righteous as being the people who belong to the right God, the God of righteousness, truth, freedom, justice and equality of the nation of righteousness.

Today, the so-called Negroes must be resurrected and made to know and understand the fate of anyone who will follow or be deceived by the arch-deceivers.

The strongest and most powerful weapon the arch-deceivers have at their disposal is to deceive the world of righteousness (the Nation of Islam). They do not stop at the common, ignorant Muslims, but reach also for the scholars and scientists of Islam, who should be aware of their trickery and deceit.

We are in a world that is passing out of existence - and she is putting up a fight (war to destroy the Nation of righteousness). Be aware! To try to oppose the success of Allah's truth, only means the doom of falsehood and its teachers.

The world of evil makes its first attack on the world of righteousness, thereby clearly showing herself as being the enemy of righteousness. When she thinks she has built up a strong force to attack the righteous, she does so which, as I said before, hastens her own doom. Falsehood cannot be victorious over the truth in the day of truth. The resurrection is a day of truth, as it triumphs over falsehood.

The arch-deceivers force war against themselves. Their ultimate aim is to do as their people always have done - try to destroy the preacher of truth and those who believe and follow him. This was the aim of Cain when he slew his brother, Abel, and the aim of the dragon when he sought to destroy the woman (the Messenger), as it is written in Revelation 12:4.

THE LOST FOUND members of that nation should be taught to know the ultimate aim of this world. God has visited them, and has prepared a Teacher (in myself) to teach them, thereby making it easy for them to understand and recognize this world and its secret, ultimate aim. It is even in the Bible, in Revelation 12:9. There, it speaks of the members belonging to the righteous nation, and shows that through deceit, satan causes them to become as himself - against the truth, peace, justice, safety and security one would enjoy if only he were not deceived.

Under deceit, the weak minded - who have no understanding or knowledge of the arch-deceiver, (the devil, satan) - are made preys in the hands of the arch-deceiver. This will bring about war as a showdown between the God of righteousness and the god of unrighteousness (the devil). It already has begun.

God must fulfill His promise to show Himself as God over all the powers of heaven and earth, and men on earth. As it is written (Thessalonians 2:9), He comes after the workings of satan has been given power, knowledge and authority to deceive as many as he could before the appearance of God or the universal manifestation of the presence of God. He was given this power in the beginning, according to chapters 2 and 7 of the Holy Qur'an, and according to the Bible in Genesis 1:26, Revelations 6:4,8 and Revelations 12:3,4.

We have known all of our lives that the devil was a great deceiver and enemy of God, and that he wished to be the victor with his knowledge of superior arts in deceiving the people of God.

He desires to cast them down, disgrace them and make them accept his deceit before the very face of God in the general resurrection of the dead.

The so-called American Negroes - as I have repeatedly taught in the articles, sermons and lectures to my people - are the spiritually dead. They have been touched and paralyzed to death by the arch-deceiver through his missionary teachings, his literature, his personal conversation and by accepting his advice. God has given to me a very strong and invincible truth that will defend, protect and prevent you from falling victim to the arch-deceiver. Read these articles, and treasure them, they are your life. Ignore them, and it is your death.

Peace...Peace...

AL-FARD *THE DAWN*

THE MUSLIM PROGRAM
WHAT THE MUSLIMS WANT

This is the question asked most frequently by both the whites and the blacks. The answers to this question I shall state as simply as possible.

1. **WE WANT freedom.** We want a full and complete freedom.

2. **WE WANT justice.** Equal justice under the law. We want justice applied equally to all, regardless of creed class or color.

3. **WE WANT equality of opportunity.** We want equal membership in society with the best in civilized society.

4. **WE WANT our people** in America whose parents or grandparents were descendants from slaves, to be allowed to establish a separate state or territory of their own - either on this continent or elsewhere. We believe that our former slave masters are obligated to provide such land and that the area must be fertile and minerally rich. We believe that our former slave masters are obligated to maintain and supply our needs in this separate territory for the next 20 to 25 years-until we are able to produce and supply our own needs.

Since we cannot get along with them in peace and equality, after giving them 400 years of our sweat and blood and receiving in return some of the worst treatment human beings have ever experienced, we believe our contributions to this land and the suffering forced upon us by the white America, justifies our demand for complete separation in a state or territory of our own.

5. **WE WANT freedom** for all Believers of Islam now held in federal prisons. We want freedom for all black men and women now under death sentence in innumerable prisons in the North as well as the South. We want every black man and woman to have the freedom to accept or reject being separated from the slave master's children and establish a land of their own.

We know that the above plan for the solution of the black and white conflict is the best and only answer to the problem between two people.

6. **WE WANT an immediate end to the police brutality** and mob attacks against the so-called Negro throughout the United States. We believe that the Federal government should intercede to see that black men and women tried in white courts receive justice in accordance with the laws of the land or allow us to build a new nation for ourselves, dedicated to justice, freedom and liberty.

7. As long as we are not allowed to establish a state or territory of our own, we demand not only equal justice under the laws of the United States, but equal employment opportunities- NOW!

We do not believe that after 400 years of free or nearly free labor, sweat and blood, which has helped America to become rich and powerful, that so many thousands of black people should have to subsist on relief, charity or live in poor houses.

8. **WE WANT** the government of the United States to exempt our people from ALL taxation as long as we are deprived of equal justice under the laws of the land.

9. **WE WANT** equal education-but separate schools up to 16 for boys and 18 for girls on the condition that the girls are sent to women's colleges and universities. We want all black children educated, taught and trained by their own teachers. Under such schooling system we believe we will make a better nation of people. The United States government should provide Free, all. Necessary textbooks and equipment, schools, colleges and buildings. The Muslim teachers shall be left free to teach and train their people in the way of righteousness, decency and self-respect.

10. **WE** believe that intermarriage or race mixing should be prohibited. We want the religion of Islam taught without hindrance or suppression.

These are some of the things that we, the Muslims, want for our people in North America.

ALI MAHDI MUHAMMAD

THE MUSLIM PROGRAM
WHAT THE MUSLIMS BELIEVE

1. **WE BELIEVE** in the One God Whose proper Name is Allah.

2. **WE BELIEVE** in the Holy Qu-ran and in the Scriptures of all the Prophets of God.

3. **WE BELIEVE** in the truth of the Bible, but we believe that it has been tampered with and must be reinterpreted so that mankind will not be snared by the falsehoods that have been added to it.

4. **WE BELIEVE** in Allah's Prophets and the Scriptures they brought to the people.

5. **WE BELIEVE** in the resurrection of the dead--not in physical resurrection--but in mental resurrection. We believe that the so- called Negroes are most in need of mental resurrection; therefore, they will be resurrected first.

Furthermore, we believe we are the people of God's choice, as it has been written, that God would choose the rejected and the despised. We can find no other persons fitting this description in these last days more than the so-called Negroes in America. We believe in the resurrection of the righteous.

6. **WE BELIEVE** in the judgment; we believe this first judgment will take place as God revealed, in America...

7. **WE BELIEVE** this is the time in history for the separation of the so-called Negroes and the so-called white Americans. We believe the Blackman should be freed in name as well as in fact. By this we mean that he should be freed from the names imposed upon him by his former slave masters. Names, which identified him as being the slave master's slave. We believe that if we are free indeed, we should go in our own people's name-- the black people of the earth.

8. **WE BELIEVE** in justice for all, whether in God or not; we believe as others, that we are due equal justice as human beings. We believe in equality--as a nation--of equals. We do not believe that we are equal with our slave masters in the status of "freed slaves". We recognize and respect American citizens as independent peoples and we respect their laws, which govern this nation.

9. **WE BELIEVE** that the offer of integration is hypocritical and is made by those who are trying to deceive the black people into believing that their 400-year-old- open enemies of freedom justice and equality are, all of a sudden, their "friends". Furthermore, we believe that such deception is intended to prevent black people from realizing that the time in history has arrived for the separation from the whites in this nation.

If the white people are truthful about their professed friendship toward the so-called Negro, they can prove it by dividing up America with their slaves.

We do not believe that America will ever be able to furnish enough jobs for her own millions of unemployed, in addition to jobs for the 20,000,000 black people as well.

10. **WE BELIEVE** that we, who declared ourselves to be righteous Muslims, should not participate in wars, which take the lives of humans. We do not believe this nation should force us to take part in such wars, for we have nothing to gain from it unless America agrees to give us the necessary territory wherein we may have something to fight for.

11. **WE BELIEVE** our women should be respected and protected as the women of other nationalities are respected and protected.

12. **WE BELIEVE** that Allah (God) appeared in the Person of Master W. Ford Muhammad, July 1930; the long awaited "Messiah" of the Christians and the "Mahdi" of the Muslims.

We believe further and lastly that Allah is God and besides HIM there is no God and He will bring about a universal government of peace wherein we all can live in peace together.

A MUST READ!
The Future Master Fard Muhammad
By
The Most Hon. Elijah Muhammad

He, Elijah said, *"I have been made equal in knowledge with Allah. I control the winds and the seas. I have power over the sun, moon and stars. I have waited 379 years for this day."* -1960 Saviour's Day Speech (Chicago, Illinois)

Order Now!
New World Nation of Islam
PO BOX 8466
Newark, NJ 07108

$12.95 + $4.25 S/H +$1.00 Tracking Number = $18.20

ON-DEMAND EPISODES

FEATURED SHOW

LISTEN TO THE LIFE SAVING TEACHINGS OF THE MOST HONORABLE ELIJAH MUHAMMAD AS TAUGHT BY THE NATIONAL SPOKESMAN OF THE NEW WORLD NATION OF ISLAM, MINISTER MUMIN ALLAH.

LISTEN EVERY FRIDAY FROM 6PM - 7PM
FOR QUESTIONS EMAIL:
SPOKESMAN@NEWWORLDNATIONISLAM.COM

WWW.THENEWWORLDNATIONOFISLAM.COM

LISTEN LIVE AT:
www.blogtalkradio.com/new-world-nation-of-islam

AL-FARD *THE DAWN*

OTHER BOOKS WRITTEN BY ALI MAHDI MUHAMMAD

Seven Steps To Allah God

First Academy

English Lesson C-2

AVAILABLE NOW

Uncle Yah Yah $14.95

Uncle Yah Yah Pt 2 $19.95 (Hardcover)
Uncle Yah Yah Part 2 $14.95 (Paperback)
S/H $4.25 for one book $7.00 for both

New World Nation of Islam
PO Box 8466
Newark, NJ 07108
www.thenewworldnationofislam.com

email your sales questions to:
admin-order@newworldnationislam.com

NWNOI PUBLICATIONS

The Future Master Fard Muhammad
ISBN:978-0-9890425-0-5
Publication Date: 2/1/2013
Avaliable Now $12.95
Send Orders to:
NWNOI Publications
PO Box 8466
Newark, NJ 07108

Knowledge of The Gods
ISBN:978-0-9890425-2-9
Publication Date: 4/28/2015
Avaliable Now $16.99
Send Orders to:
NWNOI Publications
PO Box 8466
Newark, NJ 07108

AL-Fard: The Dawn
ISBN:978-1-947732-17-9
Publication Date: 4/10/2018
Avaliable Now $16.99
Send Orders to:
NWNOI Publications
PO Box 8466
Newark, NJ 07108

S/H $4.25 for 1 book, $6.25 for 2 books, $9.25 for 3 books

ALI MAHDI MUHAMMAD
FIELD SUPREME MINISTER OF THE HONORABLE ELIJAH MUHAMMAD

WRITE OR SEND DONATIONS TO: THE NEW WORLD NATION OF ISLAM
PO BOX 8466 | NEWARK | NEW JERSEY 07108

SEND DONATIONS VIA PAYPAL: DONATENEWWORLD@GMAIL.COM

WWW.THENEWWORLDNATIONOFISLAM.COM

ALI MAHDI MUHAMMAD

www.ingramcontent.com/pod-product-compliance
Lightning Source LLC
Chambersburg PA
CBHW021155080526
44588CB00008B/341